PARTY

MONSTER

A Fabulous but True Tale of Murder in Clubland

Previously published as *Disco Bloodbath*

JAMES ST. JAMES

Simon & Schuster Paperbacks

New York London Toronto Sydney

SIMON & SCHUSTER PAPERBACKS
Rockefeller Center
1230 Avenue of the Americas
New York, NY 10020

First Simon & Schuster paperback edition 2003

SIMON & SCHUSTER PAPERBACKS and colophon are
registered trademarks of Simon & Schuster, Inc.

For information about special discounts for bulk purchases,
please contact Simon & Schuster Special Sales at
1-800-456-6798 or business@simonandschuster.com.

Designed by Ruth Lee

Manufactured in the United States of America

13 15 17 19 20 18 16 14

The Library of Congress has cataloged the hardcover edition as follows:

St. James, James.
Disco bloodbath / James St. James.
p.   cm.
1. St. James, James. 2. Narcotic addicts—New York (State)—
New York Biography. 3. Drug abuse and crime—New York (State)—
New York Case studies. 4. Drug abuse—New York (State)—New York—
Case studies. 5. Murder—New York (State)—New York Case studies.
6. New York (N.Y.)—Social conditions. I. Title.
HV5805.S7A3   1999
364.15′23′097471—dc21   99-21858

ISBN-13: 978-0-684-85764-0
ISBN-10:   0-684-85764-2
ISBN-13: 978-0-7432-5982-8(Pbk.)
ISBN-10:   0-7432-5982-3(Pbk.)

Previously published as *Disco Bloodbath*

To Harvey

Author's Foreword

Gentle Reader,

Galloping alongside this gripping murder mystery, this *true* murder mystery—is the running commentary of a babbling drug addict—me—and the outpouring of my consequential experiences with the drug Special K. It's a ghoulish tale, told with brutal candor, and it's not for the faint of heart or the weak of stomach.

But if you've paid your money and jumped on board—and you really want to get to know these people I've laid in front of you, and understand the choices they made—you'll need to know something about this drug called K.

Otherwise you'll be lost in sauce, as they say.

So let's start at the very beginning (a very good place to start . . .)

KETAMINE HYDROCHLORIDE is actually:

2—(2—Chlorophenyl 1)—(methylamino)—cyclohexanone hydrochloride
M.W.—274.2 $C_{13}H_{16}ClNO$-HCl LD50 (IPR-MUS): 400mg/kg, LD50 (IVN-MUS): 77 mg/kg
White solid with a melting point of 266°C.
Its water solubility is 20g/100ml.
And it's not flammable.

It's an anesthetic used primarily for veterinary purposes—although there are unconfirmed stories of its use in the fields of Vietnam, when on-the-spot amputations were required. It blocks nerve paths without depressing respiratory and circulatory functions, and therefore acts as a safe and reliable anesthetic.

It's a *dissociative* drug, and I'll get into that later, but—PAY ATTENTION PLEASE—*it selectively reduces excitation of central mammalian neurons by N-methyl aspartate.*

So basically, it fucks you up.

It's hard to explain, but it bends your thoughts into a non-linear, looping sort of format . . . it *pretzels* your thoughts into Möbius strips; you see everything inside and out and curling all around itself.

It's a powder; you put it up your nose.
But first, it comes in a liquid form, in a lovely little bottle

with a yellow label, and you should struggle to open it for a good sweaty hour.

Then you cook it. In the oven.

Now, you might be asking yourself, *"How long should I cook my K?"*

Experts have been debating this matter for centuries. Some say: Air Dry. Some say: Steam Dry. The Net says: Microwave. I have one friend who insists upon *an incubator*—although I'm just as mystified by that one as you.

Now, I'm not up on your laws of thermodynamics, but *I think I have it figured out.*

I usually set the oven at 250°.

Then:

Recite the "Once more unto the breach, dear friends" scene from *Henry V.*

Four minutes of bun-tightening exercises.

Knit, knit, purl. Knit, knit, purl. (*Work on that afghan for your mother.*)

Then, I have a little medley of show tunes I've cleverly clipped together, to while away the gestation period. I always start with "Rose's Turn" from *Gypsy.* Then a little *Brigadoon*, a bit of *South Pacific* (I recommend "Some Enchanted Evening" over the rather more obvious "I'm Gonna Wash That Man Right Outa My Hair" . . .)

During the *Flower Drum Song* interlude, I check the oven and tap one foot impatiently, keeping beat to the horn section that is building up to a pulse-pounding, mind-blowing, show-stopping, no-holds-barred rendition of "Bless Your Beautiful Hide" from *Seven Brides for Seven Brothers.*

Most likely, it's ready now.

It's magic time. Scrape the Pyrex, grind it into powder, then . . . up and away!

PARTY MONSTER

Special K.

It's a **clean smelling** trip up the nose.

You wait twenty seconds.

Then, there is the roar of a jet engine, so you lie back and wait a while longer.

Close your eyes and it's a whole new world.

There's a lot of *unfolding*. Everything just slides away, like many curtains opening at once.

And your *muscles* hallucinate—they feel lifted upward, quickly, so your stomach drops. Nothing can prepare you for that up, up, up feeling—when you're on the ceiling, and the ceiling keeps getting higher.

You are borne upon a wave, and pushed upward and forward.

And then: eyes—open.

But they've been open.

You're in the K-hole now.

When you focus, you look around the room—but is it the same room?—do you know this room? It may seem ultraclear, or hot and shadowy, or '50s kitschy . . . and then it changes.

The set changes . . .

a quick turn of the floor and . . .

There's a Moroccan influence, or a slick and modern approach, then it blends back into what it is—until it shifts again.

K is a displacer—you are outside of your head, and everything, *everything,* is new. You must look at that couch for the first time—define what it is—make a connection—and that's hard.

For some strange reason, that couch looks like a *dancing*

tree frog. Not literally, like an acid hallucination . . . but subtly, so you can see both, the couch *and* the tree frog existing at once.

Now if you face the hallucination, and acknowledge it, you can change that frog into, say, a can of corn. The couch is still there, but now *it looks just like a can of corn.*

It's the damnedest thing.

The room changes, quickly, and . . . where was I?

Eyes closed, because something wondrous is happening. The universe is decoding itself to you, and even though nothing makes sense, it all comes together—and if you try to think about it, it's gone again and you're back on the ceiling sitting on your can of corn.

Welcome to the land of K.

MARCH 31, 1996

MARCH

THERE ARE TIMES,
when the drugs are flowing and the emotions are running high, the lights and music can make you dizzy—and the world slips out of control.

It's like a car accident that happens too quickly . . . you can't stop it, you can't think about it, you just have to lean back, and watch as everything changes forever.

You've lost control, you say to yourself, as the wheel of the world slips from your hands—"It's happening too fast"—and all you can do is wait for the ride to end, the car to crash, the world to stop.

It's like chasing after time, chasing after the things that have already happened, because the drugs have made you too slow.

*You're thick and awkward, but if you can just catch up, then maybe
you can grab it, maybe you can grab at time and stop it—*

But no.

It's already happened.

You have no choice. Play it out.

*That's how Michael described to me the moments leading up
to the murder. That's the way he described killing Angel.*

I didn't realize when I came over to his house to warm my
feet that we would be having such a serious conversation. I must
confess, I was rather unprepared for it.

You see, my night had started off very typically . . .

When I surfaced from my K-hole, I didn't know *where* I was, exactly, but that's not unusual. I didn't recognize anybody, either,
but that, *too*, is not unusual. Often on Special K, everybody looks
like Mrs. Butterworth—all clear and brown and syrupy slow. It's
usually quite comical to watch them pour over each other and
on to each other, then ooze across a dance floor.

I panicked, though, this time, and bolted from whatever
club I was just in—too quickly perhaps.

I was barefoot and without a coat. I was wearing . . . hmmm,
what was I wearing? Goodness! I guess I was wearing a *peignoir*—
not at all suitable for a blizzard in Times Square.

But yes, by the looks of it, I was in Times Square, nearly
naked, in half-drag, and those spots in my eyes were snowflakes.

I didn't have any money and, for the life of me, I couldn't remember where I lived. And the club I had just left? It had already disappeared.

A sticky situation.

I stumbled through the storm until I came across a police station.

The doors were locked, so I knocked, and when an officer opened the door, I boldly announced that I was turning myself in. "I would like to be taken into custody immediately, please. I'm very cold."

Strangely, they wouldn't let me in. "Please, sirs, I'm sure I've done all sorts of illegal things this evening. We can work out the charges later. Now about that one phone call . . ."

"There's a phone booth on the corner," the officer growled and locked the door on me again. "Go away, you."

I had to beg for change, and New Yorkers proved to be a callous lot. Maybe it was that my eyes were going, lizardlike, in two directions. Maybe it was my potbelly spilling out of the filmy little negligee that I was wearing. But nobody stopped to help, which was just as well: I didn't know my phone number, anyway.

I sat down in a puddle to cry.

Then I looked up and saw a beacon of hope. Miles away, but there. A point of reference—Riverbank! My old home. My fortress of solitude. Michael's home now. I can go to Michael's! I can go home to Riverbank!

I hobbled through the snow, with a little string of snot swinging from my nose in the frigid night air. I had only a few rocks thrown at me on the way.

The doormen, God Bless Them, remembered me and let me go straight up. Michael's door was open, wide open, but nobody was home. I sat down and inspected my battered little body for frostbite and chilblains—and I don't even know what chilblains are.

But I was safe.

Safe and sound on friendly ground.

I took a quick look around, and was surprised by what I found. Since when, I wondered, did Michael Alig ever show any interest in home decorating? When did he get taste? He'd always been *alarmingly unoriginal,* as far as I was concerned.

But this! It wasn't Brooke Astor's taste, to be sure, or even mine, but his apartment had undergone a rather radical transformation in the months since I'd last seen it. A decent Louis Quinze replica rested in the corner, a marble bust of some mad composer in the foyer, a red velvet sofa with golden claws and ram's head arms . . . Not bad. Little glass drug vials filled with colored liquids dangled prettily from a new chandelier and tinkled in the night air.

Very odd.

He clomped into the apartment and when he saw that I was there, threw his arms around me: "Skrinkle!" he cried.

"Oh! Hey, Skroddle . . ."

"Lover-la-da, I'm so glad you're here. We have so much to

catch up on. Would you like some tea?" he asked. "Here, come get nice and comfy."

We went into the bedroom and climbed onto his big new bed. He put a Bergman film (*Wild Strawberries*? Michael was watching *Wild Strawberries*?) into the new VCR on top of his new television, that sat next to his brand-new computer. *Something was very wrong here.*

"Michael, you can't even read. What on earth do you need a computer for?"

"Oh . . . ah . . . it's a . . . gift for Freeze." He waved his hand dismissively. "Scone? They're from Balducci's . . ."

I shook my head no. Then he got out nine bags of heroin and lined them up on the tray next to the tea cozy.

I reached for a bag and he slapped me.

"After. I want you coherent for this. Now try the tarts."

We nibbled and sipped and giggled like geese.

Then twenty minutes later . . .

"James, we have to talk . . . Do you notice anything different? Anyone missing?"

"Missing? From this room? I don't get it."

"No, just missing in general. A drug dealer who hasn't been seen in a while?"

"Freeze?"

"No, no, no. Another drug dealer. Used to stay here . . ."

"Freeze stays here."

"The *other* drug dealer who stays with me. I hate it when you do Special K."

I shrugged thickly.

"Angel, James. Angel. Haven't you noticed Angel hasn't been around?"

Angel? *Ech.*

I mean, well, sure, I *guess* Angel was a drug dealer . . . oh, but he was the **worst kind** of drug dealer: *the kind who actually wanted money for his drugs.* How rude is THAT? So, I avoided him like the plague, of course, which wasn't easy. He strutted around the clubs like he was God's Own Cousin, sporting a ridiculous pair of wings, yes WINGS. Dingy old white wings, that were always knocking off my wig or spilling my drink. Oh, he was such a nightmare!

"No, Michael," I said, "I haven't seen Angel lately. I don't care enough for him to keep track of where he is. In fact, you really ought to get rid of him. He makes you look bad. He's so nasty. And those wings are so damn annoying . . ."

"Oh. Well, you'll be happy to hear that I did **just that.** I got rid of him, all right." He laughed in that staccato, half snort and gulp that is uniquely his. "Yep, I got rid of him, boy, **once and for all.** Skrink-la-da-doo! *I killed him."*

I didn't believe it at first. He was exaggerating, I thought. Something happened, of course, something always happens.

Oh, Angel probably was dead, all right. No big deal. Or maybe he was in the hospital. Who cared? They had probably been partying too hard and Angel overdosed. Happens all the time. People die around us all the time. Drop like flies. Overdose. AIDS. Sometimes they kill themselves. People come. They go. Dying is the same as rehab or moving back to Missouri. It just means I won't be seeing them again. New people were already in line to take their place.

Hey ho. I grabbed a bag of heroin.

"Please, James. This is serious."

I could tell that he really was upset.

So he told me the whole story, from beginning to end, how he and Freeze had murdered Angel during a fight, and how they dismembered the body and threw it into the Hudson River.

There is a fight, an argument. Each one contends, in turn, that *he is owed money. Michael, of course, has been robbing Angel blind for months, stealing his drugs, dipping into his profit margin. Everybody knows it. Angel knows it, but because Michael is his idol, he has chosen not to say anything. Until now. Suddenly, he wants it back. He wants it all back. Michael is outraged. Angel owes **him** money, he says, Angel owes **him** rent.*

Such a confrontation would have been inconceivable just a few short weeks ago. Angel wouldn't have dared.

But times have changed.

*The fight escalates. They're both angry, out of control. Michael is like an ape-child who doesn't know his own strength, who frequently bites and draws blood, who doesn't notice—doesn't care—**feels justified in fact,** and is oblivious to the pain and discomfort of others. Michael, the ape-child, punches Angel, or kicks him; he's petulant, angry, not about the money, not about the argument, but about the shift in power. Angel is fighting back and that means Angel is lost to him forever.*

Angel has been empowered, you see. There had been another fight, an earlier fight, two days before, in which Angel finally stood up to Michael. It was a first, and a precedent was set: he can fight back, so he does. He pushes Michael up against the wall.

Things are happening quickly now.

At this point Michael's roommate Freeze walks in. With
Daniel. No, that's not right. Maybe Freeze walks in alone. Maybe
Freeze wakes up when Daniel arrives, or maybe Daniel wakes up when
Freeze walks in. Who can tell? Michael's story changes with each
retelling. The official story, though, according to the newspapers, is
that a boy named Daniel was asleep in the next room when Freeze
entered the living room. So Daniel is asleep and therefore not a part
of what happens next. Got that? Here we go.
      Freeze then leaps into the fray, although this is unlike any
side of Freeze that I've ever seen. Freeze, who is detached,
emotionally unplugged and unavailable, who floats in and out of
people's lives so carefully, quietly, always, so as not to disturb the
balance of things, so that he may come back again and again and
nobody will mind——**this very different** Freeze leaps into the fray to
help Michael. Apparently, just this once, he felt compelled to muster
up some energy, bring himself to care. Maybe he thought of Michael
as his last chance, the last person who could possibly help him, and
he sought to protect him. Or maybe he had been freebasing again
and that accounts for the energy and the anger it must have taken,
because a freebasing Freeze is an evil mother-fucker.

      At any rate, help arrives.
      Like all faggots who fight, there is kicking and screaming and
much Mary-ism involved. Nelly little girls grab the first thing they
see and use it.
      Michael needs help, fast, just grab something and use it,
swing, connect, hurt, like anybody would.
      Freeze took a hammer and hit three times, knocking Angel to
the floor.

There are times when the world slips out of control. It's like an accident that is happening too quickly, and you can't stop it, you can't think about it, you have no choice but to lean back and watch as everything changes forever.

All you can do is wait for the ride to end, the car to crash, the world to stop.

You're chasing after time, chasing after the things that have already happened, because the drugs have made you too slow. You're thick and awkward, but if you can just catch up, you can grab it, you can stop it—

But no.

It's already happened.

You have no choice but to play it out.

And they see what's happened.

Roll the film.

There is blood everywhere and Angel is down. His head is open.

In one of Michael's versions of the story, Angel does not go quietly into the night. The dead man made a reluctant corpse. He seizes, he seizures, he tries to make it to the door. He looks to Michael for help—**He looks to Michael for help!**—even utters those words. He is confused, hurt . . . Does he know that it is about to end? Can he think clearly, can he comprehend the enormity of what is about to happen—or has his mind short-circuited with the last blow?

(In a later version, he screams and they muffle those screams with a pillow. This may or may not have been true, although it is important to remember that he mentions doing this only later, and then just as an aside. **Neither one of them knew that asphyxiation was the official cause of death.** They learned that with the rest of the world after the body had been examined. Which means, they were operating under the assumption that he was still with us when they . . . when they . . .)

He's down. He's hurt. Not moving now. Call the police? Call an ambulance? Ah, but the need for self-preservation is stronger than you think. Angel is over. Angel is no more. If he lives he will most likely be brain-damaged or a vegetable. He may be paralyzed, comatose—something is very wrong. Will somebody **please** pick the brains off the floor? Something awful, something irreparable has happened to him. If he were to live, if they were to call the police— he may be in a coma for the rest of his life, for the rest of **their** lives. They would be responsible **forever** for what has happened.

It is far easier to rationalize, in that state of mind, that they are doing the humane thing. They are putting him out of his misery. He is in pain. **Let's get it over with.**

And it will save all of us, the rest of our lives, having to care for this vegetable, cripple, or whatever.

So how do we do it—

I'm not going to do it—

Well, I'm not going to do it—

You do it—

You're the one who hit him over the fucking head—

I was helping you, asshole—**Goddamn it, we are in this together—**

This is what is happening now—this is how it's playing out.

Not me, not you—I'm not going to do it. **We'll both do it—**

Now this is how it's done, this is how it's done in the movies, on TV. Anyone who has ever grown up watching Columbo, Quincy, Cannon, Charlie's Angels—this is what murderers do . . .

They make a pact. They will do it together. They are bound together forever.

How to do it? There's a needle:
"Maybe a heroin overdose?"
"Good God, man, how could you even suggest such a thing?! We're going to need that. In fact, let's all do a bit right now, just to think clearly."

They do, and a method crystallizes.

OK, now get the Drano.
From the kitchen.

Find a vein, and insert your needles. At the count of three, I want you to push into Angel's body the steaming, acidic mix of caustic lye and sodium silicates. Try not to look at his eyes, and notice not the tears that flow down his cheeks. Never mind the terror and the pain and the confusion he feels. Look away from the betrayal and the death. Never mind the future, never mind yourselves.
One,
Two,
Three.

There is a final flash of pain; his body arches, leaps upward, eyes open, accusing.
And it's all over. For Angel it's all over forever. For Michael and Freeze—only five minutes have passed but five minutes that changed who they were forever.

PARTY MONSTER

What next? How now?

Unfolding in front of us is a scene so chilling, so horrific, so utterly bizarre that if you look real close and real fast—you can actually see Alfred Hitchcock in the background, cleaning the windows.

Look at this. Look at them: Two wild-eyed dope fiends huddled around **ye olde corpus delecti,** needles poised, Drano drained.

Blood is everywhere. Torrents of blood spilled into the hallway. A trail that starts in the living room pushes its way into the hall, past the kitchen. Almost to the door. He almost made it out the door, almost free, almost lived, but he was stopped, a third blow to the head, or a pillow to the face. Whatever.

Sticky red footprints in a grotesque dance pattern—left foot, left foot, right, right, right . . . Handprints smeared on the wall . . . little blue clots of something like jelly, stuck in the floorboards . . .

As the horror dawns, as they realize what they've done, a vague unease settles upon them . . . far off . . . not yet formed . . . not yet understood, are the troubles they face . . . But for now, one thought, one voice:

"How easy it was."

How simple. Anybody could have done this. There is no mystery to death. No complicated pattern, nothing difficult. They are not special. It could happen again. Anytime. Anywhere. Of course. A slight miscalculation, a simple mistake—it didn't take a special kind of person. Death was easy. A piece of pie. That is the true horror.

So now: action. A call to order. A caucus. Murderers unite.

The exact words, the exact blocking, is blurry. The minutes of that meeting are lost forever. I do know that Michael panicked and called Peter, his boss, for help—Peter who has **always** helped, who was magic that way, and pulled strings that don't exist for the rest of us—he called Peter but was denied access by Peter's girlfriend, Alexandra.

"Leave us alone," she said. "Click," she said.

Three times they called, and three times they were denied.

What to do? What to do?

I know Freeze became unhinged, going on a crack binge of superhuman proportions.

Watching at the window.

Waiting.

For the police. For Angel's ghost.

For a long time he was silent, watching the snow of that terrible winter sweep along the terrace.

"I don't know what you're talking about."

"You're fucking crazy."

This, whenever Michael tries to talk about what happened. Whenever Michael starts complaining about the smell, the body.

But horror fades whereas comedy endures.

Michael bounces back with breathtaking elasticity. Within hours, it is business as usual.

He stashes the body in the bathtub—to let fluids drain.

They go shopping. Invite friends over. Many friends. "Never mind the stench, pass me a straw."

Like a lousy, lopsided Lucy episode, a girl goes in the bathroom to pee, and a mottled arm tumbles out from behind the shower curtain—"Oh, excuse me!" she says, "I didn't know there was anyone in here." And she quickly hurries back to the party.
Needless to say, that bathroom is blocked off—a mattress is leaned against it—and that smell? Plumbing problems . . .

Finally, how long has it been—a week? almost two?—and something must be done . . . That bloated, gaseous, purple corpse must go!
Freeze is no help: "This is your problem, Michael."

I suppose they argue, but finally it's up to Michael to chop off the legs. It's the only way he'll fit in the box.
A bargain was struck: Freeze would go to Macy's and buy the cutlery required to dispose of the remains. He would also provide Michael with enough heroin to do the job.

*"Fuck you, Freeze," Michael said as he inhaled an unprecedented ten bags of heroin, "I hope I overdose and die and then you have **two** bodies on your hands. I hate you for making me do this."*
But once the inevitable is accepted, this, too, is not so bad. Fortified by the warm blanket of dope, and swept up in a Technicolor B-movie fantasy, he takes to his task like Leatherface at Thanksgiving.

"Was it hard to do? Did you have to hack at it?" I asked.
"No, no, no. It was like cutting chicken. The meat just fell

off. And the bones snapped really easy." Then he showed me the ordinary kitchen knife he used.

Who was this person in front of me, I wondered yet again, but I reminded myself that person is me. There but for the Grace of God . . . opposite ends of the same stick . . . and all that . . .

And that was the story **as he told it to me that first night,** except for a few loose ends.

Like instead of taking the almost always empty service elevator at Riverbank, they take the trunk down the main elevator, sharing it with an older gentleman who couldn't help but comment on the smell.
. . . past the security guards and doorman, bless 'em . . .
And then, via taxi, to the pier across the street from the Tunnel. After both bags of legs sank nicely to the bottom, they tossed in the box. But, of course—oh those wacky club kids— comedy ensues when they realize the trunk was **lined with cork.**

They couldn't do anything except watch as Angel floated off to his sweet reward.

Yes, kids, Angels float, and **that** *was his ultimate revenge.*

Of course, as he was weaving this tawdry little tale, my world was ending.

My head fell into one of those spinning cartoon vortexes . . .

The room was lurching and heaving about, the floor would drop, the ceiling cave in. Spikes popped out of the walls and the walls inched closer together . . .

I was frozen in an adorable Macaulay Culkinesque pose, with my mouth wide open, throughout.

No, I did not respond to all of this with my usual élan. Nothing could ever be the same. I was no longer the same naive waif blowing sideways through life. My wide-eyed innocence was gone, and within the space of that half hour, I was transmogrified into the bitter, broken hag you see before you.

Michael had finally gone too far. In one fell swoop—no, make that *three fell swoops*—he destroyed **everything** . . . everything he had worked so hard to create. And now: the party was over. The ride was through. It was the end of an era, MY era, and, *damnit*, that meant I was about to become "dated." *Talk about adding insult to injury!!*

"My goodness," I finally managed, as I collected the clumps of hair that had fallen from my head, "that's quite a story."

"Does this change your opinion of me? Do you love me less?"

(A difficult and, well, rather unexpected question, given the circumstance. Really best to sit down and think about it another day.)

"Of course I love you, darling," I replied automatically. Then: "It's just that, well, *you're Michael Alig*, I've always known you were capable of really big things . . . monumental . . . historical . . . things—"

"Oh—that is so sweet!" He air-hugged me, then added: "*And you're James St. James, don't forget!*"

"I know, dear . . ."

And we gave each other a quick social peck.

"My point was . . . I just . . . I mean, why waste your big chance at immortality on Angel? He was so inconsequential. He wasn't worth it! You couldn't have taken out Bianca Jagger? Rubbed out Courtney Love? You realize that everything from now on is changed—because of **Angel?** What a waste."

He looked almost humble for a moment.

"I need a bag rather desperately, Michael."

"Well, I'm glad you're finally addicted . . ."

"Oh, I'm not. *Blech.*"

Heroin is such an ugly drug. Everytime I do it, *every day of my life,* I'm reminded just how unattractive it is, and how happy I am that I'm not addicted.

I sniffed one bag, just to get a grip on the situation. Disgusting stuff!

First of all, it tastes filthy. Like powdered pavement. Like your mother's disapproval. Then there's the gag and the drip, followed by . . . nothing. So of course I did more. This news was a lot to deal with.

And I just never learn when to stop.

My eyes won't stay open, but they won't stay closed, either. So it's a *tic-toc* thing, jerking, then slumping, heaving and sighing. Moaning and groaning.

No, no, no, I think. This is all wrong, I think.

None of this is right.

I'm nasty. Nauseous. Groggy. I can't pee. For the life of me.

Pretty soon I'll be vomiting urine. Then I'll need the old do-it-yourself catheter kit.

Oh, I hate heroin.

Maybe this time it will be better.
Yea, maybe I've been doing it wrong all these times.

I began slowly putting the pieces together.
"So, all this new stuff . . . the furniture, the computer . . . Balducci's . . . the drugs . . ."
"Money from Angel's bag." Eight thousand, he said. Or thirteen. Or twenty. I can't rightly recall. The heroin was kicking in and *for once* I was swept away in a warm current of sanguine thoughts.
"Wait . . . wait a min . . . ute. You mean,"—*it was registering*—"You went on a shopping spree afterward? . . . Gorgeous!"
Suddenly the whole situation seemed farcical. Slapstick. And we laughed until our sides hurt. We laughed until tears ran down our faces. "And those boots, Michael? They look awfully familiar . . ."
"Angel's."
And we collapsed on the pillows in peals of girlish laughter.
"You're wearing Angel's boots?"
. . . *more laughter* . . .
"Aren't they nice?"

Then we stopped laughing as abruptly as we had begun. "Do you still love me? Really?" he asked.

Hanging in the airspace above my head was the monstrously vain implication that I even loved him in the **first place.** Endured him, yes. Admired him? Yes . . . but with clenched teeth.

And I suppose I even got a vicarious kick from the improbable life he had always led. But it was a wistful kick, and it always made me sad, like I was in the backseat straining to see the fun that was going on ahead of me.

But if familiarity breeds contempt, it also fosters a bond—and over the years he had become family. *He has been at various times my best friend, my worst enemy, my rival, my partner, my neighbor, my boss, and my worst nightmare*—so buck him, fuck him, chomp at the bit to get away from him . . . he was still there. He was Michael. And no matter how you sliced it *(whoops)*—yes, I loved Michael, still.

"Of course, I do darling." I sighed. "Do you have any K?"

But this didn't mean I could ever accept what happened. I needed to understand it, pull it apart. I needed to synthesize the previous monster, who was merely annoying, with this new one, who was actually homicidal . . . and, more importantly, I had to look at the monster in me that could understand and love someone like this.

To do that, I had to go back. Way back, to the very beginning. My head hurt, and the crest of dope was breaking. Where was that Special K?

He poured some out and I inhaled a hefty line.

I could hear the skrinkling of Michael's new computer as the K pushed me down and carried me away. My mind splintered into a thousand fragments, then regrouped and configured as it saw fit . . .

IN THE BEGINNING

IN THE BEGINNING

there was "skrinkle," and it was good. "Skrinkle" begat "skroddle" and that, too, was good . . . unless it was bad.

"Skrinkle," and its corollary "skroddle," were the building blocks of a strange little world Michael was building for himself. It was a language of his own, and it consisted of just those two words and the infinite variations, conjugations, and not-so-subtle shifts in their meanings.

Either word could, in fact, mean anything—depending upon its context.

You were either a "skrink" or a "skrod."

I was a "skrink-la-da" if I was good. Or a stupid "scrod-lover" if I was bad.

Oh, but I'm sorry. Unless you, too, are doing Special K, then I'm going too fast, and none of this makes any sense. I guess I need to be a bit more linear. Let me start again . . .

Here's the deal:

I am responsible for everything that's happened—*every-thing!*—the good, the bad, and the ugly. Well, maybe not so much the ugly. Michael does deserve *some* of the credit.

But it all begins and ends with me.

Me! Me! Me!

I spawned Michael Alig, and for that I will forever be damned.

This is how I remember it happening:

I blew into town in 1984, from some plains state, and got off the train, looking for all the world *just like Shirley Jones in "Oklahoma!"* I was a kicky, corn-fed lass, with a song in my heart and a rosy hue on my cheeks . . .

Plucky? You bet!

I had a satchel full of crazy dreams, and a down-home country manner that people naturally cottoned to.

Why Andy Warhol, himself, took one look at me and said: "You there! I want YOU to be my next superstar!"

What are you looking at? You think I'm making this up? It's true! Go ask him!

No, really.

*Ask anybody. That's what happened. I came first. I was the orig-*inal.

So, anyway.

I'm Shirley Jones, right? All sunshine and freckles.

And if I'm Shirley Jones, that would make Michael ... well ... that would make him Danny Bonaduce, wouldn't it? *Little Danny Partridge,* the slick-as-snot troublemaker who gets away with all the good lines.

Oh yes, I like that.

He, of course, has an entirely different view of things.

To hear *Michael* tell it, I am Mr. Magoo—that crazy old codger, bumping into walls and talking to himself—who buys drinks for the sexy little lamp in the corner and feeds the end table a dog biscuit.

He would then get to be Tennessee Tuxedo, the wise-cracking penguin, who is looped obsessively onto his VCR.

So I suppose somewhere in between our two delusions lies the truth:

I guess I *am* a myopic old man in Shirley Partridge drag. And he must be a red-headed penguin.

I hope that helps.

You see, I just love analogies. *Give me a good old analogy any day.* That's what I say.

I think it's infinitely more telling for me to say that, oh, *if we were characters on* The Simpsons, *I would be Grampa Simpson and he would be Mr. Burns.*

Or if we were slices of bread, then *he's Cinnamon Raisin Swirl, I'm Sourdough.*

In chemical terms: *he's a catalyst, I'm a noble gas.*

PARTY MONSTER

How bloated we all are to think that our childhoods matter, that anybody really cares about our little lives. Nobody wants to read about your little rag doll or your first-grade teacher. I always notice a slight glazing of the eye whenever I trot out my old "pooping in the neighbor's lawn" story.

One time, while snooping through his things, I discovered Michael Alig's unpublished memoirs. In them, he goes on for an eternity about "digging a hole to hell" when he was a child, and listening to the furnace at night, thinking it was the voice of the devil. Sure it's a sweet bit of foreshadowing: we see his paranoia, his fascination with the dark side . . .

But really.

Wading waist-high in Michael's childhood memories is not my idea of fun.

So very quickly: his childhood.

I imagine it was full of, you know, pathos and pain. And there was a divorce, of course, and it was very hard on the kids . . .

He was poor. I like to think of him as a dirty street urchin, sucking on a stick. But somehow I bet he was the apple of everybody's eye—Bonnie Prince Michael—and what little the family had, went to him.

He talks endlessly about a certain "experimental school" he went to—one of those terribly progressive early '70s things—

where you went to "blue rooms" and everybody applauded when you had a bowel movement. He credits this school for his free-thinking, rule-breaking ways.

Even so, I suspect he was a Ritalin child, impossible to pin down—you know, asking "What does this button do?" after he's pushed it and the building next door has exploded and collapsed in a pile of dust. I would also imagine he seduced the neighborhood children during sleep-overs, and poked out the eyes of many a neighborhood dog.

His mother, Elka, was a blowzy Shelley-Winters-in-her-sex-pot-days, and I'm being kind here. In that attempted autobiography, if you choose to believe it, there are all sorts of juicy tidbits about her, *things you wouldn't believe.* Of course, I'm too much of a lady to go into detail here. Suffice it to say, Michael alleges that there were all sorts of comings and goings in the Alig household, a topsy-turvy little world.

The elderly couple next door, Clarabel and Earl, swooped in and took over the daily job of raising him. I'm sure he was their little gift from heaven, as they had nothing better to do, and it allowed Elka the freedom to pursue, well, "other things." Hmmm. I seem to recall there was a brief stint at catalogue modeling, ski wear and what-not, and oh! you should see the pictures!

So that's his childhood. There it is.
Yada, yada, yada.

We all have issues, we all had problems. I was no different, really. We were both boys, two boys, two Midwestern misfits. We had parallel running lives . . .

While I was getting boogers wiped in my hair during Biology, he was being spit on in Social Studies.

A common story.

But there was a day, a sunny day in May, I'm sure, when at exactly 2 P.M., we both looked out of the window of our different schools and . . . What?

We didn't wish—wishes are wasted . . .

We didn't hope—because our future was inevitable . . .

And we didn't pray—we were on our own.

So we sent out energy bullets: "This is for New York."

"This is for when I get there."

Little pockets of energy, to be saved and accumulated and used upon arrival.

I can only project my longings and my needs onto him. I can only express my *rapture* in finding an *Interview* magazine, seeing a picture of Andy Warhol or Divine, and just *aching*.

I was so scared it was all going to be *gone* by the time I got there. Ninth grade, tenth grade—can't this thing go any faster?

In the magazine, there were funny people with funny names like John Sex, who had wild white hair and a snake!—and didn't that just open up a kaleidoscope of new possibilities?

And how long the years are—endless! And the minutiae of your daily life! So tedious, when there are BIG THINGS happening a thousand miles away. And when you go to bed at night, it's hard to believe those people, those fabulous, daunting people, are out there right now!

So we wait, and we endure, and someday **we will be there,** and **we will make it.**

And, by golly, we did . . .

The club scene that I arrived onto in the mid-'80s was an impenetrable clique, with a complex hierarchy of "superstars." There were intricate rules of behavior, Byzantine rituals, and unspoken customs that were designed to exclude the unwanted, and massage the egos of the Chosen Few.

There was a certain type of person who was deemed "fabulous"—but only if that person understood the system's infrastructure and played by its rules.

At the tippy-top of this system was the nightclub **Area,** the downtown society magazine *Details,* and the titular Queen of the Night, **Dianne Brill.** The goal, then, was to have your picture in *Details,* with Dianne, in the VIP Room of Area. If that happened, well, **God himself would drop out of the heavens and give you a drink ticket.**

It was a tough nut to crack, I'll tell you that much.

But for someone, like myself, who had all the time in the world, and a closet full of flowing lamé things, it seemed like a perfect way to while away the evenings.

I took to my task with the plucky determination of a Perfume Sprayer at Bloomingdale's. Nothing could stop me. I was like a rabid MCI operator—oozing sincerity, feigning "spontaneous" conversations, and always, but always, just right there in your face.

Oh, I had moxie, all right. Like Pia Zadora on a sugar rush.

I enlisted the aid of a buxom young girl, to counteract my sometimes unnerving flamboyance. She was my sidekick. My partner in crime.

I schooled her in the Art of Schmoozing.

I even went so far as to make up flash cards to help her remember who stood where in the social scheme of things.

"Who's this?" I asked, as I held up a laminated card.

"Cornelia Guest!"

"Very good. Now what's her dog's name?"

"Mr. Whiskers."

And then, when we would actually SEE Cornelia out and about, well, we were her BEST FRIENDS! We would hug her and kiss her: "How is Mr. Whiskers?" and she played right along, too embarrassed to admit she didn't know us from a hole in the wall.

I learned very quickly, watching the master, Dianne Brill, at work. She was brilliant. And now I will pass her ancient secrets on to you. Here, for the first time, is the Art of Working a Room.

Now you, too, can conquer any scene in high style! Watch as uppity faggots fall into line! Semi-important people think that you're a Somebody! Has-beens cling to your coattails! It's easy! It's fun! It's the patented Brill-o-matic 1-2-3 to Social Acceptance!

First: Spend at least six hours getting ready. Study yourself in the mirror at home. Is your hairdo media-friendly? Will your outfit read in black and white? Does your "look" inspire at least two clever sound bites?

Remember, you must be eye-catching but simple. If you and your "look" can be reduced to a simple caricature and not lose any essential qualities, you've got yourself a hit. Think **Carmen Miranda. Jessica Rabbit. The band members of Poison.**

Be sure that your partner doesn't clash with your look. Plan ahead and execute together.

As you stand outside the entrance to the party, take your partner by the hand and shake it once for solidarity. Quickly, adjust your vibrations to the music. Throw your ears back, push your energy forward, turn on that smile and **SWEEP** into view.

Enter the room in a clatter of commotion.

Circle the room, once together, smiling and saying hello to **EVERY PERSON** in the room. Even if you don't know them. **ESPECIALLY** if you don't know them. Pretend that you do. You should make a snappy comment about something they're wearing: "My what a beautiful corsage!" (if it's a woman or a drag queen); or "Darling, look at those massive shoulders!" (if it's a man or a drag queen).

Smile and acknowledge **EVERY PERSON** in the room . . . in a clockwise rotation—never stopping, never pausing—always moving, always smiling . . . brilliant . . . animated . . . **ON!**

This takes twenty to twenty-five minutes.

Then: Separate!

Both of you circle, alone, in opposite directions. (You continue moving clockwise, your partner retraces your steps.) Pretend you are searching for each other—that it's a matter of life and death—and be sure to involve *every person* in the club in your desperate hunt.

(This should take no longer than twenty-five minutes.)

Finally, regroup and scream with transcendental bliss at the thrill of finding one and other again.

Now, lock arms and work the whole room again, telling all your newfound friends, "Not to worry, we've found each other at long last."

Then leave.

Never stay longer than an hour and a half. And that is on the very outside. I MEAN IT!

Always leave them wanting more.

Do this every night, for three months, at the hottest club in town, and I personally guarantee that for the rest of your life you will know everybody in every room of every party, everywhere.

That's what we did. We climbed our way into their charmed little circle. Me and my booby best friend were dubbed "celebutantes" by *Newsweek* magazine, and soon we were the toast of the town.

Now, if you're looking for some sort of lofty moral summation—like: "Being Popular Isn't What's Important"—well, you won't find it here. Because I had a **wonderful time** . . .

... met a lot of fascinating people ...

... and saw sights that would make Caligula blush ...

And I also learned some VERY IMPORTANT LIFE LESSONS.

For example:

- If two or three people of equal social standing are posing for a photograph, you always want to stand ON THE RIGHT of everybody else. That way, in the picture, you will be first on the left, and the caption will read: "James St. James and Blah Blah Blah were seen at . . ."—So psychologically, you get top billing.

- Once something appears in print, **it automatically becomes true.** Ipso facto. If a columnist says that you are an ugly baboon with two noses and a spastic colon—well then, prepare to live out the rest of your life that way. Nobody will ever believe otherwise.

- Contrary to popular belief, there *is* such a thing as bad press. Just trust me on this one.

- Which leads me to the most important rule of all: **Never, ever dish anyone in print.** No matter who they are. No matter how many looks they've stolen from you over the years. No matter how many times they've humiliated you at dinner parties, or peed on your pant leg. If somebody asks you for a quote about your mortal enemy, simply drip with sincerity as you gush: "I worship him." And leave it at that. IF YOU'RE CORNERED AND YOU **HAVE** TO TELL THE TRUTH, AND THE TRUTH IS, WELL, SLIGHTLY BITCHY, put a positive spin on it, then quickly follow it up by giving three reasons why you're even worse. **FOR EXAMPLE:** "Sure, Michael is a monster—**but look at that flawless eyeliner!** How many monsters do you know that can wield liquid liner LIKE THAT? Besides, I have anal fissures. And I just love Captain Lou Albano. Oh, do I have bad breath? Here, smell . . ." Works like a charm.

That's what I learned when I was fabulous.
What does it all mean? Not much.
It qualifies me to be a hostess at Denny's.

But, remember—at the time, I took it all rather seriously. I paid my dues. Played by the rules.

There I was, sitting pretty, perched in the upper branches of the nightclubbing hierarchy.

Suddenly, in **whooshed** Michael Alig—just as *brazen*, just as *devil-may-care*, just as *uncouth* and *unschooled*. . . .

A big old bowling ball searching for a gutter . . .

I remember I was at the bar at Area, coolly studying my reflection in a Doublemint gum wrapper that was lying there. More lip gloss, perhaps?

That's when he came skroddling up to the bar. I saw him and I thought, *My Lord, that could **very well be** my uglier twin sister!* He had the same pigtails, same lunchbox, same fashionable blue lips! It was unnerving!

"Hi. I'm Michael Alig. And you're James St. James!"

"Well. I'm glad we finally got that worked out."

"I saw you on *Oprah* and I have your picture from *Interview* magazine on my refrigerator."

"Of course you do, darling. Now, if you'll excuse me . . ."

"I'm going to be a party promoter."

"So is my Guatemalan housekeeper. But you hang in there, dear. Goodbye."

"What do you think of this idea: a masquerade party at the Kit Kat Club where everybody comes dressed as their favorite Saturday morning cartoon character, like Electra-Woman or Hong Kong Phooey?"

"I'd rather have rectal cancer, darling, but it was sweet of you to ask. Now, *goodnight*."

And I ran for the exit, hoping that was the end of it.

But there he was again, the next night—draped across *Village Voice* gossip columnist Michael Musto! And the next night, and every night, every party, everywhere we went—THERE HE WAS! Smiling and chatting up everybody in the room!

Well, everyone was just horrified!

Of course, I ignored him. Who wanted some *loud, young upstart*, just brazenly walking up to total strangers in a club, acting as if he knew them!

How crass! How contrived! Did he think we didn't see through his blatant social climbing?!

There are a million stories of how we all tortured him, ran from him, and tried desperately to thwart him. When he was a busboy at Area, I might throw drinks and ashtrays on the ground and scream "Busboy!" just to make him grovel. When he started throwing parties at Danceteria, we wouldn't be caught dead gracing them with our social presence. He wasn't written about in *Details*. He was simply not allowed in our clique.

There was only one reason I maybe tolerated a moment or two of his presence *at all:* I was madly in love with his boyfriend: The future Superstar DJ, Keoki.

When they met, Keoki was still a baggage handler for TWA. He somehow got into Area one night and met Michael, who was still a busboy. They were both very different people then from who they are now. This was before the egos, the drugs, the successes, the failures, and the fans. But maybe they saw the future in one and another. Who knows? Who cares. Anyway, they left together and embarked on an eight-year, whirlwind, co-dependent, psychotic love affair.

Little Keoki was just adorable back then. Cute as a bug. I was immediately smitten. I remember we all were. The entire club stopped cold the first night Michael brought out his hot little Spanish boy-toy.

How could *he* get someone that cute?

But there he was, and there they were. Keoki was in his underwear on a mattress in the corner of the lounge at Area. I don't remember why. Perhaps Michael had gotten him a job as an Art Installation. Or maybe he just felt fabulous.

But here was this gorgeous, Dionysian, creature, a real Latin heartthrob, smothering MICHAEL ALIG in kisses.

We were flummoxed.

Absolutely flummoxed.

And so, I was in love.

Now maybe, *if I look real deep into myself,* I can admit that *just maybe* I have a few intimacy issues that need to be resolved. I mention this only because I dealt with my "crush" just like any ten-year-old would: I chased him around and tortured him mercilessly. If he had had pigtails, I'd have pulled them.

Michael launched an elaborate campaign to secure a job for Keoki at Area. Keoki decided he wanted to be a DJ—despite the fact that he didn't know the first thing about it. *Oh, he was just awful.* His selections were a mishmash of the pretentious, the obvious, and just plain bad taste. Nobody could clear a room faster than Keoki.

Nevertheless, Michael began billing him as "The It Boy of the '80s" on every flier for every party.

"The It Boy of the '80s"?

Ludicrous!

How could I not make fun of that? Nobody even knew who he was!

But I did go on a bit. Anytime he walked into a room, I would scream, *scream:* "OH MY GOD! IT'S THE 'IT BOY'!"

I was braying like a herniated yak.

Every night—"IT'S THE 'IT BOY'!"

Until one night, he was go-go dancing in his underwear, and Michael and I stood transfixed, unable to stop ourselves from gawking. Then, abruptly, I launched into my tirade.

"LOOK AT THE 'IT BOY'!"

But Keoki had had enough. He grabbed a drink from the bar and began pelting me with ice cubes. Cube after cube, *CLUNK,* on my head, *CLUNK,* down my shirt. Ice cubes were followed by lemon wedges, and before I knew it, I was being pummeled with cigarette butts and beer bottles, OH THE HU-MANITY!

The other go-go boys joined in. Spurred on by Keoki's taunts and jeers, they poured drinks on me, seriously staining my pretty new tube skirt, I will never forget it.

I fell to the floor, racked with sobs. How could somebody so beautiful be such a monster?

Another time, Musto and I were posed in our corner of the Palladium bathroom with our force fields **UP**. We were saying deeply superficial things to each other, and looking very soigné doing so. Nobody would have dared to approach us. We were that good.

Nobody, except . . .

Leaping and **bounding** through the crowd—arms flailing, invites spilling everywhere—looking for all the world like Old Yeller in heat . . .

MICHAEL ALIG!

He **dared** enter our sacred personal space! He was out of breath, panting, and looking positively CANINE, in some weird furry sort of getup. He poked his face *RIGHT INTO OURS*, as if it were the most natural thing in the world, something he did every day.

"JAMES! MICHAEL! MICHAEL! JAMES! Oh My God! Hi! I AM SO GLAD I FOUND YOU! I'm throwing a party, you *have* to come! It's at Area and the theme of the party is BLUE. Doesn't that sound like fun? Can I put you down on the YES list, please?"

I'd rather suck a urinal cake.

"I'll be sure to red-letter it on my social calendar," Musto gushed in that ego-squashing way of his. "I was going to go to Bianca Jagger's birthday . . . but . . . hmm . . . Bianca or Blue? Blue or Bianca? Hey, it's *Blue* for me! I'll be there!"

"No, really, guys—it's going to be fun. Open bar from ten till eleven! PLEASE? Please come . . ."

Hoping to sidestep a commitment, I quickly changed the subject.

"My, that's some jacket you have there." The jacket was *awful*. Goat fur. Or dead dog. And waist length! Simply GENIUS. So IN-YOUR-FACE. Hookers would use this jacket to blow their noses on. And it was a balmy 102 degrees in the ladies' room. Why hadn't he checked it with coat check? Or the ASPCA? "Yep, that's SOME look, there."

"You like it?" He petted the matted fur fondly, and then it dawned on me: poor dear—he wasn't being camp! He must have thought he looked *chic* . . . or *moneyed!* He was parading around like a mangy little monkey because he was *proud of this look.* This was clearly a boy going nowhere—fast.

"It was a Christmas present from Keoki. Try it on! Here! Go ahead! Really, it'll look great on you!"

Oh My God. Should I?

I could see Musto's attention span waning—any minute he might bolt. Three minutes of his time, and an original epigram to take home, was all he gave to any one person. Anything more exhausted him. Michael Alig had already used up his allotted time.

BUT THAT COAT WAS SUCH A GIGGLE! Even *he* wanted to try it on.

I was wearing leopard spandex and six-inch spikes. It would match hysterically. I slipped it on.

"Heavy Metal Housewife from Yonkers!" Musto announced, and everybody clapped. I vamped a bit, and *Michael was in heaven:* HIS coat on MY back . . . with a Musto quote to boot!

Oh, it was such an ill coat!

I looked positively *perverse*—just like Divine, only young and thin and with a pretty face.

I couldn't take it off. I struck a few more poses, until—

. . . out of the corner of my eye . . .

I saw an angry mass of manliness RUSH into the room and,

—*before I knew it*—

I was THROWN against the wall.

It was Keoki, red-faced and rabid.

"Take it off! Now! Take it off or I'll kick the crap out of you!"

Then he turned to Michael: "How dare you, Michael Alig—let him wear your *Christmas present?* And James St. James, OF ALL PEOPLE! How could you? Is this how you treat my gift? You just ruined my present!"

It was a full-blown, "all eyes on me" temper tantrum.

Musto, whose Warholian fear of confrontation instantly propelled him halfway across the club, left me to deal with this cut-rate Ricky Ricardo.

"But. I. He—" was all I could sputter.

Michael was absolutely mortified by this poorly timed and wildly distorted display of Latino *bravado*. Keoki had clearly ruined his moment—a truly *fabulous* moment of *real social bonding.* He had probably been hoping against hope that it would end up in Musto's column. But that dream was dashed. Musto was gone, I was angry, and it was most likely neither of us would come to his Blue Party! What started off ten minutes ago as one cozy stepup, was now disastrously three steps down the still rigid social ladder.

I grabbed my lunchbox and tried to pull off a huffy exit: "I guess *the It Boy* must have been VERY CLOSE to that dog when it was still alive!"

Oh, that Keoki! Here I was *doing Michael a favor* by transforming his flea-bitten old rag into a postmodern coat of irony.

I was more determined than ever to keep my distance from those freaks. Disagreeable troublemakers, that's what they were. I predicted then that they'd both be gone and forgotten in six months' time. Those types never lasted.

Our little war escalated quickly until one night . . .

Ah yes. I remember it well . . .

The opening night of the Tunnel . . . and it was going to be FABULOUS! This might single-handedly **bring back nightlife as we knew it!**

I still had my old-lady bubble hairdo—and my dear, I spent the entire day in the beauty salon: starting with a wash and mousse, setting it with rollers, under the drier, then backcomb, hairspray, tease, hairspray, curling iron, hairspray—IT TOOK HOURS.

By the time I was through, it was enormous! Über bubble!
I was Super Society Woman!

And my dress!
It was Gaultier—green and blue satin, with giant Russian
lettering, in velvet, across the chest and arms.
Too chic!
Remember that season? Fall '86 I think, and all that Soviet
madness? We wore Russian logos and listened to Sigue Sigue
Sputnik. Oh, and we all quoted Karl Marx and went to those
Yakov Smirnoff concerts (or was that just me?). Anyway, *Commu-
nist chic was all the rage.*
So, in a word, I was stunning.
And!
It was a club opening! A special occasion! **Put on your
most festive party hat!** You couldn't wait to see the same people
you saw every night, IN A WHOLE NEW SETTING!
It was almost **too much fun!!**

But there was a glitch.
A fly in the ointment.
Musto and I had agreed to present a Nightlife Award at
Area. Michael Alig was doing something called "The Glammies,"
in which he would recognize and honor those in the scene for
their contributions (GIRL OF THE MOMENT! HOTTEST GO-
GO BOY! BIGGEST SLUT!).
We **never** would have agreed to do this on tonight of all
nights, but we had agreed long before we knew of the conflict.
Who knew it would fall on the night of the BIGGEST PARTY OF
THE YEAR?
And Dianne was coming with Raquel Welch—they were
friends now!—That Dianne was such a meteor!

At least Michael was putting us on the budget and we were going to get fifty dollars apiece!

Fifty dollars just to show up at a nightclub!

What an innovation!

It worked, because there we were, at Area—AREA! Of all places! Area was already over. Very "last month." You could smell the decay.

There I was, pretty as a picture. All gussied up—new heels (patent leather, with little bows on the heel! FABULOUS! SQUEAL!).

The hairdo of life . . .

And the most fabulous dress I have ever owned!

Sitting with Michael Alig—MICHAEL ALIG!—at Area—AREA!—when the entire civilized world was across town. "If I miss Dianne and Rockie, I'll just die! Oh and Andy will be there! And Liza!"

Cut to this dreary wake.

Oh, it was too much! Fifty dollars or no fifty dollars, let's get this show on the road! Hup to it!

Well, Michael had to milk our presence for all it was worth and parade us around to the managers to show what a good crowd he pulled in.

GOOD CROWD? It was the four of us and a few crickets!

Finally the awards started—I was wound up so tight—I don't remember anything about it, except I was in an **awful** mood.

My turn. I got on stage. Someone handed me the category. "Best DJ."

Oh dear.

"And the nominees are . . ." and I read a list of the crème de la crème—the most fabulous DJs in the city (NONE OF

WHOM WERE THERE)—and Keoki (who WAS SEATED NEXT
TO THE STAGE).

"And the winner is . . ."

No. Please. No. Even Michael would not stoop this low!

"OH MY GOD!" I shrieked, "IT'S THE 'IT BOY'!"

Keoki, who couldn't mix two songs to save his life; Keoki,
who nobody knew, who was three months on the scene—Keoki
won against the tops, the most talented, the A-listers.

Wouldn't you know?

"Where's the It Boy? Somebody get the goddamn It Boy, so
we can get our money and get the hell out of here and go to the
Tunnel, PLEASE!"

And I began to stomp off stage.

Well, I went too far. From my grand old age now, and the
wisdom I've accumulated, yes, even I concede—I went too far.

I was rude and I ruined Michael's party and embarrassed
him in front of the managers he was trying so hard to impress.

But don't cry for Michael and Keoki.

Listen to what happened next, and I think you'll agree
that, well, I got my comeuppance (and then some!), and the punishment far exceeded the crime.

Keoki and two of his goons bum's-rushed the stage,
picked me up, and threw me—THREW ME!—

Like I was an old tissue!

Like I wasn't a delicate porcelain doll!

They threw me into the fountain.

And everybody laughed.

They laughed at me.

Me!

The celebutante!

And when I sputtered and crawled out of the water—

My four-hour hairdo was . . . was . . . a mop! A bunch of henna'ed noodles!

And my panty hose were bagging around my ankles!

And my pretty new dress was ruined.

I looked like . . . a soggy old sea hag!

It was the worst night of my life!

I'm getting all choked up again, just telling you about it.

I went to the opening of the Tunnel, anyway, and everybody was very sweet when I cornered them and vented and sobbed and generally called so much attention to myself that I was actually pretty fabulous.

But, oh!, that Keoki!

I was so mad at him!

I was so mad, I . . . broke down and got him a drink and we had a really long, complicated conversation about . . . my lip gloss.

And thus, in my darkest hour, out of cruelty came kindness. We bonded that night and became friends—through thick and thin—and that friendship has endured ten tumultuous years.

Sure, I was still in love with him, but now we were friends as well.

And it was because I spent so much time with Keoki that a thaw in my attitude toward Michael was inevitable.

PARTY MONSTER

But let's peel the onion here. Psychologically, I think I chose to fall in love with Keoki as an excuse. That way I could set up my friendship with Michael, and still think of him as an adversary.

I didn't have to admit to myself that I might really like him. I was free to resent him.

So I floated into their lives and it felt right and comfortable.

The old crowd was appalled with me: "There goes Troll St. Troll! Looks like he found a new bandwagon to hop on to!" "Like a barnacle in heat, that one!"

After all the ranting and raving about my dislike for Michael—and my contempt for his silly little parties—I guess I did look hypocritical.

But there I was: in a little fake fur number, doing the ropes at the Tunnel basement. A "club kid," of all things!

That's all six months down the road, though.

In the meantime, Michael's star was on the rise. Warhol died and suddenly, "going Downtown" lost its cachet. The thrill-seekers moved on. Downtown turned into a frail and weak shadow of its former self. It maybe could have limped along bravely for another couple of years. Or maybe not. At any rate, that's when Musto, who was perhaps having yet another bad hair day and feeling peevish, effectively killed the scene with his February 1987 *Village Voice* cover story: "The Death of Downtown."

Instantly the fun was over.

My celebutante days were gone. Anybody connected with the old scene was considered outdated.

Enter, the club kids.

Now, damnit, let me say this about that: I do not want to chronicle the history of the club kid movement. I have neither the desire nor the wherewithal to accomplish that. I leave it to the professionals.

Rather, I want to paint you a watercolor of my relationship with Michael—a sweeping impressionistic view of the dynamics of our relationship, and how a little thing like murder could forever alter the balance of power.

I really don't think people actually care about the nuts and bolts of nightclubbing politics, or the ever-changing cast of club kids.

Nobody really wants to hear the incredible true life stories of Jenny Go-Getter and Really Denise.

And I am **NOT** going to spend hours and pages describing in mind-numbing detail each wacky new look.

Suffice it to say: there was a group of people called the Club Kids that Michael created in his own image, and they all had funny names that he usually chose for them like—oh— "Oliver Twisted" and "Julius Teazer" . . .

And they—you know—oh, I don't know—**shoved strawberries up their nose and ran around swinging an alarm clock above their head**—and called it "a look."

Yes, the looks were pretty lame in the beginning—just cheap homemade costumes. I used to feel like my mother on Halloween: "And what do we have here? A scary monster, a cowboy, and a pretty fairy princess! Here's a hit of ecstasy, run along now."

Their sense of style got better as the years went on, but you could always spot a club kid in the wild if there was something glued to his or her face: sequins? feathers? lug-nuts? a Virginia ham? Yup. That's a club kid.

I'm not kidding.

They usually had a shelf life of six months; then they'd move back to Iowa, and become Queen of their little scenes there and forever look back on those six months as "the craziest time of my life."

So there.

That's it. The History of the Club Kids.

Enough said.

Allow me to continue with Michael's surprising rise up the ranks.

Now we all know that nature abhors a vacuum, so when the clubs were empty, Michael rushed in to fill the void.

And his parties were . . . OK . . . actually fun. Even "Blue."

I was loathe to admit it, but he had a certain energy that was undeniable.

And when, after the opening night, the Tunnel failed to draw a crowd, its creative director, Rudolf, threw his hands in the air. He had tried his damnedest to book A-list parties (Mamie Van Doren! Cornelia Guest!), but nobody wanted to go to big flashy nightclubs anymore.

It was all about the intimate. The private. It was all about a club called Nell's, where you sat on an overstuffed sofa with a bottle of claret and discussed your prostate.

Michael had been pestering Rudolf forever to let him do something at the Tunnel, and it was sort of: "What the hell, let's give it a whirl."

They had nothing to lose.

"OK Michael, you can have the basement for your little friends, and you can have the run of it. It's all yours."

And Rudolf gave him a blank check. Free reign. Go crazy! Knock yourself out!

Rudolf had a typically Teutonic sense of humor. It was a nihilistic, neo-expressionist, German-type of thing. He saw humor in ... *you know,* things like vivisection and gum disease. The sicker and sadder things got, the more inspired Rudolf became. He was perverse and decadent in a legendary sort of way. And he had a very laissez-faire attitude toward, oh, rules and morals and things. "If it feels good, do it."

Truly, Michael had found a mentor worthy of his mettle.

If Michael wanted a crazy old homeless man to do the door, Rudolf would smile and say he had his checkbook ready.

When Michael wanted to auction off, say, circus midgets or streetwalkers—well, that sounded like fun to Rudolf!

"Let's serve cat food as *hors d'ouevres.*"

"Have at it!"

Nothing was too shocking.

The Tunnel basement operated on the Chaos Theory. Insanity prevailed. There were peanut races, three-legged drag queen races, and many, many toasts made with the ever-present ecstasy punch. And the drug dealers who supplied the ecstasy were instantly acknowledged as "superstars," and became much coveted guests at all the best parties.

Michael hired all the local loons.

There was Ffloyd, the Human Money Tree: the music would suddenly stop and Ffloyd would run through the room, naked, with a hundred one-dollar bills taped to his body. He ran in one door and out the other. A free-for-all ensued and whatever you grabbed was yours to keep.

That idea proved so popular, it morphed into the $1,000 Drop. Michael would stand on a table and toss a thousand dollar bills to an often violent mob. Of course, he usually pocketed $990 and passed the remaining ten on to tip-challenged friends. But two hundred blue-faced freaks still screamed and cried and clawed and climbed to get to Michael; why, you would have thought the New Kids on the Block were masturbating on stage, the way everybody carried on.

And above it all, Michael stood and drank in the attention, smiling like the cat that ate the canary.

I remember once, Michael had a pool party and bought lots of little kiddie pools and filled them up with water, and after the ecstasy kicked in, everybody got naked.

And Michael—buoyed by all the attention, and so carried away by his own spunk—broke the main water pipes and flooded the basement until it *really was* like a pool: a giant, filthy, germ-ridden cesspool filled with hundreds of naked drug addicts.

Now if THAT isn't fun—I don't know what is!

I think Michael was given a stern reprimand for that one. He promised never to do it again. He didn't have to, because next week Lady Hennessey Brown promised to set her pussy on fire and lactate on the audience.

There was always something bigger and better on the horizon.

There was the "Celebrity Club," a weekly event hosted by three newcomers that Michael had imported from Atlanta: Larry Tee, Lahoma, and a shy, retiring wallflower named RuPaul. They were trashy and flashy and dressed in the most amazing vintage '70s outfits—when that was still a radical concept.

Each week a different "Nightclubbing Legend" (read: Old School) was named Celebrity of the Week.

It was Michael's way of getting the old guard to come to his parties, albeit one at a time.

By honoring someone like Michael Musto, he was showing the old guard who had previously snubbed him, how **fabulous** he was doing without them. I think he secretly hoped they would start crying and apologize and become club kid converts on the spot.

That never happened as far as I know.

Instead he usually ended up gushing over them for an hour or so, fawning over them to an impossible degree—and then *savagely humiliating* them near the end of the night.

He might pull off your wig, or pinch you really hard—leaving bloody welts—or he might destroy your outfit, or pee on your leg, or get on the microphone and tell the crowd you had AIDS.

Needless to say, very few "celebrities" returned for an encore.

The summer of '87 galloped by, and I'll be damned if an authentic subculture hadn't taken root and blossomed in the

Tunnel basement. That was when Michael's star really began to rise, and his creations, the club kids, took to the stage for their first appearance.

The club kids were much hated and feared in all corners of the city. You might laugh at them. You might turn up your nose at them. But after a *New York* magazine cover story with Michael smirking at you from a thousand newsstands, you talked about them incessantly. People who had never seen a club kid—wouldn't even know one if it flew up their nose—had an opinion on Michael's latest outrage or Nik Nasty's latest look.

The children had regained the night, and their enthusiasm, and the feeling that they were breaking all the rules and doing something REALLY NEW, kick-started New York nightlife.

Of course, kids dressing up and going to nightclubs is hardly groundbreaking. But to many people, it was a welcome respite from the ritual-obsessed, self-important scene that had preceded it.

I, myself, was torn. It's true that I loved the Old School (*I'm just an uppity old queen at heart*). I loved the old-time pomp and pageantry. The privilege and presumption. But, you know—by this time, *Old School was, like,* **so last season.** Really just OVER. It was either adapt or die, *and I am nothing if not resilient.*

And the kids *were* fun. They had a delightful sort of *je ne sais quoi.* What they lacked in wit and intelligence, they made up for in chutzpah and exuberance. YEAH, YEAH, YEAH, some of them were a little too perky. Annoyingly so. Preternaturally so.

But if that's the worst you can say—not a bad world to live in, huh?

Sigh.

It was all so sweet and innocent then. Your only goal was to look like a Muppet and collect as many drink tickets as possible. It was a relatively drug-free time: **heroin** was strictly for, oh, *jazz musicians* and *slumming British aristocrats;* **ketamine** was still just for cats; and *nobody could even pronounce,* much less score, this new thing: **Rohypnol.** The scene was still very oh-so-social. The worst drug calamity, the worst-case scenario, was that you accidentally took too much ecstasy and were *actually nice to a Bridge-and-Tunnel person.*

Hi-ho.

Michael was at a point in his nightclubbing career when he felt he needed to mold somebody into his special "superstar." If he was truly going to be the next Andy Warhol, he needed to find an Edie Sedgwick. He needed someone with **glamour!** ... **presence!** ... **beauty!** ... to offset him at some of the tonier parties he was getting invited to.

So he chose a terrifying old drag queen named Christina.

Mind you, Michael didn't create Christina. Nobody created Christina. Nobody could ever dream up something like her. My theory is that someone on God's Assembly Line had done too much Special K. She was an abomination of nature, like those frogs born with eyes in their throats.

PARTY MONSTER

She was a real piece of work: a crazy old buzzard with a body like Pa Kettle and a face like a hatchet . . . a bad blond wig . . . and no lips to speak of, just a thin red line . . . testicles falling well below her hemline, knocking against her knees. And pointy, stretched-out boobies from past hormone dabbling.

Her story goes like this: she was born into a good family in the Squirrel Hill section of Pittsburgh. She was a he, who was a former teacher. After some nasty allegations involving several students, the family bought him a Park Avenue loft in New York on the condition he never return to Pittsburgh and never saw them again.

That's the story, anyway. He became "Christina," a freaked-out dominatrix with dreams of Warholian glory.

She was a ticky-tacky, bottom-rung nightmare of the first degree. You'd rather swallow a bucket of snot than spend ten minutes with her.

Run, bolt, make a beeline to the door. Hide under the bar, fake a seizure, anything to get out of the room: "Oops! Anal Leakage! Gotta go!"

But she was Michael's first superstar, and for sheer shock value, she reigned supreme. She and Michael were the Wes Craven version of Edie and Andy.

She got attention, all right. In fact, she reinforced Michael's basic loathsomeness—now we wanted to hide from both of them.

It put that extra zip in our heels.

But that was just the effect Michael loved.

Because she made no sense, and because she reveled in her supposed insanity, you never knew where you stood with her. You never knew when to take her seriously.

Her steady stream of non sequiturs had a rehearsed feel—but they were unnerving nonetheless.

One night she was carrying a doll, and saying over and over in her guttural faux-German accent: "I jus haad a baby and I'm awlready zick to dess off it!" Then she would throw the doll on the floor and step on its head.

Once, in a desperate plea for the attention of her idol, she snatched Andy Warhol's wig. It happened at a book signing at Rizzoli's, and he was so devastated, he wrote in his diaries, that forever after he could only refer to it as "the incident."

Another scarier, weirder, believe-it-or-not story:

"Sometimes I kidnap leettle children and SET THEM ON FIRE!"

Oh, that wacky drag queen—what *will* she say next?

Until one night, I was at her house (I can't imagine what I was doing there) and BY GOD, IF THERE WEREN'T TWO LITTLE CHILDREN SLEEPING IN A LOCKED ROOM. Who were they? She wouldn't say. Why were they there?

Silence.

As a babysitter, she lacked a certain warm, reassuring quality. I can't imagine many parents being comfortable leaving their babies in her charge.

Certainly this wasn't Auntie Christina reaffirming her familial ties.

So what could it be? Where did she pick up two eight-year-old children?

Somehow there are things I'd rather not know. Call me irresponsible, but I'm sure there was a PERFECTLY LOGICAL EXPLANATION. Maybe she was tutoring on the side, between dominatrix gigs. Maybe they were very tired Girl Scouts, napping between cookie sales. I scanned the papers for reports of burned babies but found nothing. Oh well.

Her inability to be controlled was out of step with Michael's later "superstars," who followed him blindly.

Slowly, Christina began to unravel.

Michael threw a birthday party for her at the Tunnel, and EVERYBODY WHO WAS ANYBODY came, just to be perverse.

Michael and his minions pushed the birthday cake into her face—during the final chorus of "Happy Birthday to You"—and

POP

She snapped.

Think Carrie at the prom.

Nobody caught on fire, and we all lived, but just barely.

She snapped and grabbed a machete that she just happened to have in her handbag. Raving and swinging wildly, all covered in cake, she forced everyone in the club into a corner.

There was a standoff.

Should we laugh or should we scream? Hundreds of club kids trapped by a homicidal hag queen. Well, it sure made a nice story to tell in the locker room the next day.

It took three guards to wrestle her into submission.

This is the stuff of nightclubbing legend.

Near the end, Christina's behavior frightened off even Michael. She became increasingly violent.

The corker was a performance she gave at the Pyramid club, singing "My Funny Valentine" à la Nico.

The audience wasn't exactly bowled over by her charismatic stage presence and soaring vocals.

They booed her.

Wrong move.

She took the microphone and POKED OUT THE EYE OF AN AUDIENCE MEMBER.

Poked it out.

PLOP

The police were after her for various and sundry other infractions as well, so she was forced to move from her Park Avenue apartment. She landed at the Chelsea Hotel and spent her last days pretending to be Edie Sedgwick or Nancy Spungen or somebody.

Her last phone call was to a videographer friend who regularly videoed parties on the club scene.

"Nelson, come film my suicide."

He declined, and ten days later the Chelsea tenants complained of a bad smell coming from her room.

Thus ended a tragicomic legend. Michael lost his first superstar, but by then he had already moved on—to other superstars, yes, but also to another club, another party. A place called the Limelight offered him a job, and he accepted.

I don't think any of us could have foreseen what happened next.

Not even him.

DISCO 2000

LADIES AND GENTLEMEN! BOYS AND GIRLS OF
ALL AGES! FASTEN YOUR SEATBELTS! THE RIDE IS
ABOUT TO BEGIN! WITHOUT FURTHER ADO, I
GIVE TO YOU NOW . . . THE ONE . . . THE ONLY . . .
THE LEGENDARY . . .

DISCO 2000!

Do you feel it? The page is ablaze, these words are on fire—a whole new world is about to burst into existence!

The excitement is palpable. Are your fingers trembling in anticipation? IT'S HERE: each page richer, wilder, stranger than the last.

Michael finally had it all—the money, the dream, the space—and it was finally ready to be unleashed upon an unsuspecting world. And it was **More! Michael!** than even he could guess.

Disco 2000. The Autobahn of Nightclubs. No rules. No speed limits.

His place in the sun was finally secured, thanks to one Peter Gatien and his nightclub, the Limelight. This was the fruition of all Michael's years of work, and the knowledge and insight he had gained. That, and his uncanny intuition, and that razor-sharp third eye of his that could locate and extract the basest element in us all . . . and exploit it, ON STAGE, ALL FOR *HIS* DREAM.

Too much wasn't enough. Over the top wasn't even trying.

There was to be a weekly cast of characters. Club mascots, easily identifiable . . .

We rented animal outfits that we never intended to return—a chicken, a dog, and a bear. Those, and the banana and Coke can outfits that I graciously donated from my own wardrobe, were to set the immediate tone of the club.

The chicken, christened CLARA, THE CAREFREE CHICKEN, was to become our biggest star—*the most beloved superstar of all time!* She was tossy, saucy, and full of sass.

Clara was big and yellow, with a handsome red comb that could be construed as a mohawk if you so desired. She never said a word—*smoked a bit of crack now and again*—but never spoke a word. Her body language said it all: she danced the Funky Chicken as if to the manner born. She gave everyone a friendly peck hello. She fussed and clucked over the regulars . . . and when Keoki recorded an original song, called "Dizzy Chicken," Clara spread her wings and took to the stage.

What a chick! She was riveting! Her timing was impeccable. "Oh, that Dizzy Chicken!" It was an instant club kid anthem.

Peter made two thousand pressings of the song and used them as invitations. I still have my copy, do you?

Clara's carefree image became part of the Disco logo.

Skroddle Loddle Doo!

Then there was Hans Ulrich, the Leather Dog, who appealed to a more "select" (some would say "subversive") group of people. He may have lacked Clara's free-wheeling *joi de vivre*, but he had his own loyal band of followers—backroom boys with certain carnal kinks that he, alone, satisfied.

And I.C. the Bear—a chilly Polar dude that never really caught on with the masses. He gave up club life after only a few months and was last seen floating on a glacier in the Baltic Sea, supporting his heroin habit with a complicated scheme involving pickled herring and large-breasted Eskimo women.

But they were all there opening night.
And WHAT AN OPENING NIGHT!

The colorful menagerie of big, furry, and fantastical creatures certainly gave the club a cartoonlike aura, but this was certainly *no place for children.* Or rather, it was the ideal place for children—"Come one, come all! The Piper is calling for you!"—*just make sure Mom and Dad never find out.*
This is your introduction to the future. You're in for a wild ride. Check your soul at the door.

Like Willy Wonka at his chocolate factory, Michael pushed and nudged and planted the seeds of change. *Go ahead. Touch. Taste. Try it all, nothing is what it seems, but most likely it's what you've always secretly yearned for. Nobody will judge.*
Go ahead.
Drop those inhibitions.
Drop that acid.
Drop your pants.
Drop a few names, darling.
And please, drop a few coins into Michael's coffer.

Oh LOOK! There's me!
I'm in a cage, on the wall.
Arrows point to me and a large sign reads: "DANGER! DO

NOT FEED THE DRUG CHILD! SEE WHAT A LIFE OF SIN AND EXCESS CAN DO TO YOU! HE WAS ONCE AS YOU ARE NOW! BEWARE!"

My hair was matted, my clothes were dirty, and there were dark circles under my eyes. This wasn't a costume. But I couldn't have done better had I been working with a team of professionals.

I cried out, pitifully: "PLEASE! Just one bump! One little bump, I beg of you . . ." It was a spirited performance. I'm a stickler for Stanislavsky, you know . . . The crowd really felt my jones. I got many, many sympathy bumps, and soon enough I was so high, I broke free from my exhibit and joined the seething, liberated throng.

There were drag queens and drag kings and freaks of all kinds. Club kids in all their frippery, wearing tiaras and flower pots on their heads. Futuristic Geisha Gangsters stood next to a pair of beaded jellyfish, who were learning all about a new unisex masturbation machine made from six cow tongues attached to a rotating wheel.

Dan Dan, the Naked Man, wearing nothing but a chiffon veil, seemed to get along just fine without it. He watched as two debutantes rode Danny, the Wonder Pony around the dance floor, sidesaddle.

Woody, the Dancing Amputee was onstage, doing lascivious things with his stump, to great acclaim.

There were raver boys and pixie girls and the plucky Baroness Sherry von Koeber-Bernstein, who has been wearing a new and different plumed chapeau every night for thirty-seven years. She brought her fifteen-year-old niece, and they both po-

litely declined the complimentary lines of cocaine but happily
indulged in the buffet of Cheez Doodles and Ring-Dings that Lahoma thoughtfully provided.

Even Old School clubgoers faced up to their inborn fear
of being seen entering the once terminally tacky Limelight. But,
by gum, they filtered in and gawked and gaped with the rest of
New York.

Michael had done it.

We still debate whether or not Dianne Brill bestowed her
trend-confirming décolletage on opening night. Michael insists
that yes, she was there, and she was simply bewitched by the rav-
ishing muscle man in my banana suit.

I think it's more Dianne-esque for her not to gamble on
what could turn out to be a colossal bomb. After all, the Limelight had *never* been hip, and Michael was still considered rather
nouveau. No, she wouldn't chance it. She would man the switch-
board the following day and study the reviews with a magnifying
glass, before she **plotted out the strategy for her multimedia
covered entrance** that would insure the club's position in the
Pantheon of Painfully Hip.

I never saw her there that night, and I would know—*the
metal plate in my head vibrates if she's anywhere in the immediate
vicinity.* Trust me, I would have hunted her down and drooled on
her toenails. She wasn't there.

But Quentin Crisp *was* there, and he was shocked, I think,
by the parade of streakers who wiggled and jiggled their way
from bar to bar.

I think that when Michael is on his deathbed, and he
looks back on his long and staggeringly varied life, this, *all of*

this, will be the moment he holds dearest to his heart. The joy he felt on this, the opening night, will be his last living comfort.

And I believe I was just as happy for him and his success as he was.

Watching him, as he beamed and bantered and tossed about a never-ending supply of drink tickets, he never stopped moving and he greeted each and every person with a personalized bit of patter, whether he knew them or just pretended to. He circled each room twice and firmly stood to the right in every picture, thus assuring psychological top billing.

He was now at the tippy-top of an impenetrable clique, with a complex hierarchy of superstars. He understood the intricate rules of the system's infrastructure, and reveled in the game.

Michael Alig, bless his little black heart, was now the establishment.

Now, Michael will have you believe it was his party that single-handedly opened the mind of the world and ushered in the all-accepting '90s.

I don't know if I'd go THAT FAR.

He did give a few flashy drug dealers and a handful of bedraggled old drag queens their fifteen minutes of fame.

And Disco 2000 certainly let a whole generation of teenagers see homos and weirdos and sickos *up close and per-*

sonal, in all their majesty and splendor. And they learned that often times the very same kids they pick on in high school are the ones holding the drink tickets, the drugs, and the guest list at the coolest club in New York City.

And maybe it caused them to rethink just who the "cool ones" really are.

And certainly many, many trends started with the club kids. Although, try as I might, the fake nose fad I pushed for several years, never caught on. And, thankfully, no one bought into Michael's "feathered genital" idea. And he eventually stopped painting those damn blue dots on his face! FOUR YEARS OF BLUE DOTS! And he is still convinced it might catch on any day now.

Certainly the outlandish looks we cooked up didn't fly in Peoria. But it was the *gist* that trickled down. Colored hair, platforms, "cyber punk," piercings . . . Think Dennis Rodman, and you'll realize "trickle down" isn't necessarily a good thing.

With such a hot potato in his hands, the pressure was really on. He couldn't afford to fumble now. He had to top each new week, with MORE! MORE! MORE!

He placed an ad in the *Village Voice* looking for freaks with unusual talents.

This is perhaps my favorite image of Michael. I like to picture him behind a desk, in lederhosen and bifocals, looking down the line of bearded ladies and fire-eaters that spilled out into the hall, down the stairs, and out the back door.

No, let's replace the bifocals with a monocle, as he marches up and down, inspecting the motley crew of wanna-bes and circus rejects. Armed with a pad of paper and a keen eye for fresh freaks, he is merciless in his quest for the biggest, weirdest, wildest . . .

"Only three nipples? Grow another dozen and we'll talk!"

"Queerdonna, huh? You're a four-hundred-pound cross-dresser who lip-synchs to Madonna? Maybe you can open for someone on a slow night."

"A bearded lady? Dye it green and sit naked in a tub of lime Jell-O—we'll talk on St. Patrick's Day."

"NO, there is nothing freakish about sucking yourself off. I'm going to do it myself on my lunch hour. Don't waste my time!"

I can't remember if he ever got his dream booking: Lori and Dori, the Siamese twins connected at the head, who played country-and-western music. *Those* were the lofty heights he aspired to. *Only the best for Disco 2000.*

There were two performers he found that not only made the cut, but made nightclubbing history . . .

The first was known only as the "Pee Drinker," an apt name and an apt description of his particular forte.

Michael *loved* that. Of course, Michael loved *anything* to do with bodily functions.

The Pee Drinker would stand on stage, with his trousers around his ankles, and fill two or three plastic cups with hot . . . steaming . . . piss. Then, while the audience squirmed and winced and tried not to look, he guzzled them down with gusto. He then licked his lips, shook his penis, and took his bows.

That was considered shocking in the early days. Scandalous, even—can you imagine? How young and easily amused we were back then. Later, the poor Pee Drinker was reduced to entertaining stray Jersey girls at a back bar, drinking piss in exchange for free beer.

We were on to more sophisticated outrage by the mid-'90s.

The performance that will forever resonate in my head, the one I still can't believe, can't stop talking about, can't stop thinking about, dreaming about, screaming about, was a gal named *IDA SLAPTER*.

Just your average, typical trailer-park trannie from Austin, Texas.

Nice enough. Chatting with her at the bar, you probably didn't give her your full attention—*seen one Southern drag queen, seen 'em all*—huh? But it's those seemingly normal exteriors (the beehive hairdo, the pennyroyal house dress, the stubble beneath the pancake . . .) that hide TRULY DERANGED minds. Watch out for the average—they're usually hiding something big.

On Christmas Eve

On stage

Ida stripped naked and pulled a *full string of LIT CHRIST-MAS BULBS*, one at a time, out of her ass.

She made her way slowly across the stage.

POP! And twinkle!

POP! And twinkle!

Until you couldn't help but be swept up in the pure joy,

the awe-inspiring grandeur of the season. A twenty-four-foot string of lights coming out of Ida's butt, really reminded you of the true meaning of Christmas.

AND IF THAT ISN'T ENOUGH TO MAKE YOU PAUSE AND MARVEL AT HER SPIRIT AND DETERMINATION . . .

Listen to the whole story, from its miraculous conception to its majestic delivery.

"Light bulbs up the ass, no big deal!" you say. "On a good night I can fit a Butterball and two sweet potatoes up my bum!"

Aye—but here's the rub:

How did these bulbs come to shine so brightly? They weren't plugged into an electrical socket . . .

An hour before her performance, Ida lay spread-eagle on the ground, and she had a helping hand (*and how*) **slowly, carefully,** *millimeter by millimeter*—INSERT A BATTERY PACK INTO HER UPPER INTESTINE.

If that isn't a true showbiz trouper, why I'll eat my Ann Miller wig. And they call Gary Collins the hardest working man in show business!

And all this glorious anarchy belonged to Michael—lock, stock, and barrel. He was revered far and wide as the king. *And being king is good.* From now on, Michael is free to live in his own magical kingdom. He has the money, the connections, and the clout to indulge any of the many psychotic disorders that he calls "fun."

Close your eyes and pick one of the seven deadly sins. Now open them, and SURE ENOUGH, *there's Michael, in the middle of it.* Waving you in to join him.

And being king means that reality can simply be dismissed. And the OUTSIDE WORLD NEED NEVER TOUCH HIM. All those little things like bills and rent and food and outfits were all magically taken care of by the Patron Saint of Downtown Superstars, Peter Gatien, and his helpful staff of grunts.

Do you see a *perfectly understandable* onslaught of delusions of grandeur sometime in the near future? After all, he is lauded and applauded and rimmed clean, everywhere he goes. . . . Please note his complete inability to deal with even the *simplest* of life's problems ("blue ecstasy tonight or pink?") . . . And tell me: is that "Selective Denial" thing a blessing, or a bag on his head? . . . now dig his mind-blowing way of seeing the world: *inside out* and *from such a lofty height.* It must be rather confusing to be so savagely observant, yet stuck on a pedestal, so far removed. He has a complete and utter grasp on a world that exists only for him. And when he visits our world, he will make no concession to our customs and beliefs.

Most importantly though, note his COMPLETE AND UTTER FAITH that, no matter what: *he is the golden child, he is the chosen one,* and nothing can ever touch him. Silly little things, like public sex with a fourteen-year-old, and breaking into the neighbors' apartment to pee on their furniture . . . are magically shrugged off. It's unnerving.

And potentially destructive.

But—

That's the price you pay when you give inmates control of the asylum.

When you let the wolves guard the hen house, there's bound to be a few chicken dinners.

And when you give a psychotic infant unlimited power and privilege?

It can level a whole generation.

Among the litter, the human debris, and the wreckage of lost souls that Michael left in his wake at Disco 2000, was one Jennytalia—CLUB KID EXTRAORDINAIRE! GIRL OF THE MINUTE! NEW AGE EDIE SEDGWICK! PUNK ROCK GO-GO GIRL! EVERYBODY'S FAVORITE RIDE AT DISCO 2000!

Now don't get me wrong, *I love her to death, don't have a bad thing to say about her. She's a peach. She's a saint, that girl. But let me just say* this *about* that:

She was bald, back when that was really something.

And she pierced her own cheeks with large walruslike tusks, and, hard to believe, that too was once considered unconventional.

So she was a trendsetter.

She had a certain presence. Star Quality. She never said much, and what she did say never made much sense—but it didn't really matter. Her liquid blue eyes would fix on you, her boobs would bounce beguilingly—and you were under her spell.

Sixteen years old, and the doorgirl at the hippest haunt in town, gave her a certain cachet, notoriety.

When she appeared in a Calvin Klein ad—well, *who didn't?* It's the '90s! My great-aunt Melba was the original CK Be girl— things got crazy.

We all went to Paris one year (Michael didn't—there was a "No Smoking Crack" ordinance on transcontinental flights in those days), and Jenny modeled in the Jean Paul Gaultier show.

That clinched it for her.

She was a legend in the making.

All she had to do was follow in Michael's footsteps a bit longer, and become, in succession, a crack addict and a heroin addict—EDIE, NICO, JENNYTALIA!

But club kid stardom always takes its toll.

Who will ever forget the sight of her sitting in a trash can, trying to open a can of beans with a butter knife—because she was hungry and broke and she had given Freeze all her money so they could complete their week-long crack binge?

It wasn't all sequins and cocktails, kids.

One day I wandered off somewhere, and got a little lost. Through an extremely odd set of circumstances, I ended up in Miami Beach working as a shoe salesman. *But, that's another story entirely.*

When I returned to my senses and came back to New York, I found that Disco 2000 was still hot, and Michael was still on top, but the scene had changed. It was darker and druggier than I remembered. Heroin had made its comeback, and Special K, Rohypnol, and GHB were everywhere. Coke and ecstasy were considered passé—dinosaur food.

Now it was all about being super sloppy and out of control. The looks to look for were: "Damaged" and "Plague-ridden." *Sores and bruises. Ripped and ragged outfits.*

I guess in order to stave off boredom, the now terribly jaded club kids had resorted to massive self-destruction. They went to great lengths to shock and disgust the public at large.

Contrary to popular opinion, Michael didn't champion this change. In fact, I think it rather frightened him. Up until the early '90s, he was a control freak, who only dabbled in a bit of ecstasy now and again.

That was then.

Nowadays, the only way to stay in with the in-crowd was to play their game. Had he resisted, he would have been left behind with the other '80s relics.

So, in the beginning, he would take a bit of something here, a sniff of something there, and greatly exaggerate their effects.

"Oh ho! Look at me!" and he would fall down, very proud of himself, indeed.

He painted circles under his eyes and bruises on his body to fit in: "Look, I'm just like you!"

"I'm a crazy drug addict!"

But then something began to happen.

He stopped and listened and found the demons in his head were quiet, quelled. Heroin shut them up.

There are people who contend that it was the drugs that drove Michael mad.

I think the drugs held him together a little bit longer. He was already mad. He was always insane. He escaped into drugs to keep the monsters at bay.

Speaking from experience, there are people who have too much space between their ears, and given the time, do nothing but free fall forever inside their heads.

It's a spooky thing to be left alone inside an angry inner-verse.

Drugs redirect the fall. They cushion it. Give you a parachute. Or maybe just a flashlight and scuba gear. I don't know how you look at the inside of your head—what metaphor you choose—but for those of us with endless yawning stretches of interior and nothing but nothing to stop us from getting lost in it, drugs can be wonderfully helpful.

PARTY MONSTER

For a time.

Sure, with Michael, near the end, they exacerbated his downfall. But for many years, they cushioned it. And the downfall was inevitable, believe me. He was crazy to begin with. The drugs just made the ride more fun.

If we're all going to hell in a handbasket, we might as well make it a party on the way down.

STRANGE INTERLUDES

Now.
I think I have it.
Here.
In a nutshell.
Michael encapsulated.

Seven quick stories—seven very different stories—separated by years, and degrees of importance. Bite-sized bits of lunacy and dementia. Each vignette serving to highlight an aspect of Michael that I think is relevant to the murder of Angel.

I believe it was Nietzsche—or maybe the Desi Monster—who said that every degree of power involves a corresponding degree of freedom from good and evil.

I think after I tell you these anecdotes, I won't have to prattle on anymore about "MICHAEL'S UNIQUE PERSPECTIVE" and "HIS MISPLACED NOTIONS OF RIGHT AND WRONG." Or "MICHAEL'S LACK OF FEAR" and his "COMPLETE INABILITY TO GRASP CAUSAL EFFECTS."

Here we go. Very quickly.

STORY NUMBER ONE

We're throwing an outlaw party at the Burger King in Times Square. At midnight. Burger King has not, as yet, been informed . . . but three hundred of downtown's A-listers *have been informed,* and honey—THEY ARE DRESSING TO EXCESS.

Michael has decided that the next "BIG THING" in fashion should be EXPOSED and ACCESSORIZED genitals. *It's the natural progression of things.* So, he is naked except for a blue nose and a whimsical arrangement of sequins and feathers neatly attached to his *rather vivid* . . . uh . . . nether region.

"Butt cracks, areolas, and gangly testicles should all be allowed the same fashion options and subsequent media coverage as the rest of the body!"

So let it be noted. So let it be done.

It was all part of a well-thought-out manifesto and accompanying fashion layout in the next issue of his magazine—*Project X.* And tonight he was testing his theory.

And, my, he DID STAND OUT.

Outlaw parties are surreal events. When you take a hundred freaks out of their cozy, comfy context, and place them—

PLOP!—smack dab into reality, *without the benefit of dramatic backdrops and throbbing disco lights and, most importantly, A SELECTIVE DOORMAN,* well, their innate silliness is amplified a hundredfold.

Watch Desi Monster order a hamburger:

They can't understand a damn word he is saying, what with the muzzle he's got on . . . and he can't *see* that they don't understand because he is wearing a slotted mask that only allows a severely restricted field of vision. And his ten-inch platforms mean that he is only seeing a small, two-inch-by-one-inch section above their heads.

Hilarity ensues as HE gets frustrated, THEY get flustered, and dozens of un-invited restaurant patrons gather to poke and laugh and gawk and gape.

Now: fill the whole restaurant with similar happenings and visuals and understand why outlaw parties are such anticipated and talked-about events.

Interacting with the real world, *en masse,* and watching the real world's reaction to the spectacle we provided—*sometimes violent, sometimes amused, ALWAYS slack-jawed*—well, it's more fun than sitting at home writing this book, I'll tell you *that.*

And for Michael to stand out in this carnival of freaks *is quite an accomplishment, indeed.*

But everybody is just floored by the whole decorated genital concept. And **ESPECIALLY** Michael's bedazzled and bedecked equipment.

There are others at the party whose genitals Michael has

dressed up as well...but they don't have the—charisma?— *GIRTH?*—to carry it off with such aplomb.

Michael was drunk from all the attention.

Staggeringly drunk.

So after we all *thoroughly* trashed Burger King's upstairs dining room, and the cops came to stop the fun and arrest us all, Michael hops into a cab and tries for a clean getaway. The cab-driver, unfortunately, will not have anything to do with Michael. It's company policy to discriminate against indecent freaks.

When Michael steadfastly REFUSES to get out, the cab-driver LEAPS out of the cab and tries to physically remove him. Michael cannily locks all four doors, leaving the mad Muslim stuck outside, banging on the window.

For some reason, the trunk of the cab is open, and the driver produces a set of golf clubs (?!?). He breaks the cab window and begins beating Michael senseless.

Bleeding profusely, Michael leaves the cab and stumbles blindly home—TEN BLOCKS AWAY, THROUGH TIMES SQUARE AND HELL'S KITCHEN, with only a few sequins decorating his urethra and a mangy old turkey feather bobby-pinned to his pubic hair.

He somehow makes it back to Riverbank West, his home, where we are neighbors.

Once inside, he vomits, then passes out in the lobby, still bloody and naked.

It took two doormen and a delivery boy from across the street to carry him upstairs.

He came to, briefly, when his next-door neighbor—an elderly Asian woman—came out crying, "I can no more take this!"

"Shut up, ya old battle-ax, or I'll shut you up MYSELF!"

quoth Michael, and he raised a fist, which sent her scurrying back to the safety of her apartment.

STORY NUMBER TWO

As the club kids grew in number and notoriety, Michael was often asked to throw parties at other clubs around the country. He would then gather up as many drug dealers as he could find, grab a couple of cute Brooklyn boys, and, HURRY! Get them on the plane, put 'em in a housedress, maybe glue a clown nose on them, and then pass them off as "New York club royalty."

"What's your name again?" he'd whisper, as they arrived at the club.

"Matt."

"Oh . . . uh . . . this is Matte Lipstick . . ." he would grandly announce to the club owner, "one of New York's reigning super-stars . . ." And they loved it.

It was unnerving to discover, after one or two visits, that soon, every city in America had a growing population of club kids, comprised mostly of little Matte Lipstick wanna-bes.

I hated those trips.

I vividly recall one time—*well, it's no wonder I'm an old drunk . . .* Here. Gather 'round now children as I tell you a story.

This is a harrowing tale of *beating the odds* and *desperate times calling for desperate measures.* **Just how far will a man go to get his way?** Here is the "Strange but True Story of Flight 452 to Chicago" . . .

11:00 A.M., and the plane leaves at 11:40.

And I am a *stickler* for punctuality.

PARTY MONSTER

Don't look at me like that. It's true. I am a *fiend* when it comes to being on time. Growing up, we had to be at the airport *two hours* ahead of time. That's just the way it was.

And now Michael wouldn't wake up. We jumped up and down on his bed, we poked sticks up his ass. Nothing.

At 11:10, he got up and ordered breakfast from the deli downstairs, as I stomped and screamed and turned into my mother: "That's it! We're late! We'll never get there! Might as well unpack! Thank you for ruining my vacation, Michael!"

11:20, he started packing.

"Oh! So, now Mr. On Time has decided to get it together! Tell me, Michael, do we have time for a stroll through the park? Shall I fire up the tea kettle? Let's all play a quick hand of bridge!"

I scowled and pointed my bony finger of doom at him: "IT'S TOO LATE NOW! Might as well catch up on my Christmas thank-you notes! We'll never make it!"

11:25, we were on the road, FOR ALL THE GOOD IT WOULD DO US. I was a seething cauldron of rage.

"Stop the cab." Michael screamed to the driver.

He then hopped out and went to make a phone call as I, you know, breathed fire and spit tacks.

We got there, though, and miraculously the plane was still there. We are twenty minutes late. Michael didn't seem surprised. He wasn't surprised an hour later when we still hadn't boarded.

"What's going on?" I asked a jumpy-looking stewardess.

"Bomb threat," she said, with a twinge of hysteria in her voice. "Somebody called in a bomb threat."

We all turned to Michael, who smiled proudly. "I told you we'd make it on time."

The next day, it was on the cover of the *New York Post*.

Meanwhile, passengers on the 11:40 to Chicago, leaving several hours later than its departure time, were compensated by an all-out club kid extravaganza they will probably never forget. There was a runway show down the aisles, a vogueing battle, drugs consumed off the seat-tray tables (which should have been in their upright, locked position). There was a spirited debate over who it would be more fun to fuck: Macaulay Culkin or Emmanuel Lewis (that would have been my choice). A heavy hail of peanuts rained down on most all of the passengers. And of course a few dozen cocktails were consumed before takeoff (by me—Oh, my nerves!).

Before we made our final descent into the Windy City, Michael and Karlin Supersonic decided to steal the emergency oxygen tanks in the rear of the plane.

"It's a fabulous cyber look!"

"We'll charge people for gulps of air at the club, and tell them it's all the rage in New York."

I don't remember how they thought they were going to smuggle their contraband off the plane. The tanks didn't fit into a lunchbox. And they might look conspicuous down their pants.

The crew foiled their plan, though, before they could give it a whirl.

"Nobody is getting off this plane until the culprits confess and return the oxygen tanks!"

Two hundred angry passengers turned to our little section.

It obviously wasn't any one of the sweet Midwestern couples onboard. They had all long since had strokes, after Michael showed everyone the scabs on his penis.

Outside the plane, police cars were waiting with swirling lights.

Michael and Karlin sheepishly gave up, and the rest of the passengers were allowed to disembark.

The police still wanted to talk to us.

"Hey! Aren't you Michael Alig? From the *Geraldo* show?" they said.

I AM NOT MAKING THIS UP.

Then: "Didn't we arrest you for breaking into Al Capone's vault and having a party there, last time you were in town?"

They patted him on the head affectionately. "Now no more monkeyshines out of you, mister!"

They laughed and got back in their cars.

Oh, those wacky club kids!

STORY NUMBER THREE

Now we all know how much Michael **LOVED HIS LEGOS.** Like nothing else on earth.

He loved his Legos *so much* that he would **FLY TO GER-MANY** once a year *to visit the original Lego factory,* where he could purchase the NEWEST and RAREST Lego paraphernalia.

No half-hearted hobby THIS! No siree! GO THE DIS-

TANCE! TO THE EXTREME! You have to admire that in a person, right?

And one year—it must have been winter 1989—he happened to be there on a Lego-buying mission when they took down the Berlin Wall.

So he was a witness to history.

But being a witness was never Michael's way. He *needed to be a part of it.*

Now, I'm sure MOST of the people relocating from East Berlin to West Berlin were hardworking, honest folk. Salt of the earth. GOOD PEOPLE.

But Michael noticed an inordinate number of amoral young Easterners SURGING across the border, eager to live a life of *Capitalistic Excess.* DRUGS! SEX! MONEY! FAME!

They would do ANYTHING to purge themselves of the dreary world they had left behind.

So, of course, Michael scooped one of them up—a sweet young thing, still wet behind the ears—and took him out, showed him off, fed him drugs, and showed him the MYRIAD OF POSSIBILITIES Michael's world had to offer. He decided to take him back to New York with him and get him a job at the Limelight.

And that's when he got AN IDEA . . .

Now . . .

If all these *hot, horny, HIGH-SPIRITED, and EXCESSIVELY ENTREPRENEURIAL boys* wanted to get out of Germany and do drugs and have fun and didn't care WHO they had to fuck to do it. . . .

. . . And if Michael knew lots of wealthy old reptiles who would love *nothing more* than to have a naked East German houseboy, and didn't mind a little bit of miscommunication and occasional kleptomania . . .

WELL, WHAT COULD BE BETTER THAN SETTING UP A SERVICE TO BENEFIT BOTH PARTIES? The hustlers would get to live in America with socially connected men who would *gladly* cover a few vials here and there *if it meant they would have hot, young flesh to squire them around town.*

It was a WIN-WIN situation!

Michael and his hustler friend took Polaroids and phone numbers of lots of cute underage boys to bring back to America.

Then Michael went through his Rolodex.

That Michael was heading up a ring of underage virtual white slaves to be sold into a life of prostitution, never even entered his head.

He was just trying to make everybody happy. Laws were silly and old fashioned and just put there to ruin everybody's good time.

IT WAS UP TO HIM to break these laws for the good of the people.

Of course, none of it ever worked out. Michael's boyfriend was so smitten with our *demon Western civilization* that upon arrival in America he quickly became a junkie-klepto nightmare. Michael and Keoki had to give him the boot. He cashed in the plane ticket back to Germany that they had thoughtfully provided, and he went and bought lots of drugs and disappeared forever.

And the logistical nightmare of Michael's scheme meant that very few other people followed through with it, either. Visa problems, etcetera. One poor man tried, and he, too, was burned badly.

But this just goes to show you: *with Michael, it's the idea—not the execution—that lets you glimpse into his mind and really almost understand him.*

STORY NUMBER FOUR

You always remember your first overdose.

Other turning points in your life—your first words, your first step, your first wet dream—may be more important, but who can remember them? **But your first overdose.** Now *there* is a story that can be trod out time and again. It's appropriate at nearly all social functions. You can tell it with **glee** to your old drinking buddies. You can tell it with a **wry, ironic tone** to impress that cute little nephew of yours when his mother leaves the room. Or you can **shed a few crocodile tears** when addressing your recovery group.

Everybody enjoys a good overdose.

Especially other drug addicts. They love to steer any and all conversations toward past drug glories. They speak wistfully of stomach pumps and ambulances. With cannibalistic zeal they eagerly devour tales of "bottoming out." No humiliation should be spared when telling them the particulars of your case. Any and all degradation will be licked up and picked clean by wild-eyed compatriots who remember *only too well.*

And so it is. The time has come for me to share my first overdose with you.

Coincidentally, it's also my first experience with Special K. But that is almost incidental. In fact, it doesn't even count, because I didn't enjoy it.

But I tell this story now not to impress, or show regret, or even share a chuckle, but to illustrate how far the pendulum had swung in my relationship with Michael.

Remember the reverential way he treated me in our early days together? GONE. Gone the way of Stacy Q and men in pearls.

During this period, when he was flushed with nouveau-superstardom, he took special delight in picking at my scabs and finding new ways to humiliate me. We were still best of friends, we still had moments of great fun, and there was no denying the preternatural way we could connect on certain mental planes.

But still, it was payback time. Listen:

I was at the Palladium to judge some silly contest. I had had a bit too much to drink perhaps, and I found myself in a bathroom stall telling someone (I don't know who) that my biggest fantasy was to try a nine-inch line of Special K off of a ten-inch dick. *What a surprise to find he had both!* I happily indulged myself with shameless gusto.

But like the old 1930s Hays code in Hollywood, where no crime goes unpunished, I, too, was made to pay for my excessive behavior.

That last snootful of K must have been a doozy because immediately after taking it, the world burst into a brilliant but complex series of geometric patterns *so elaborate* that no mere mortal could even BEGIN to comprehend their true significance.

Only God and I understood—and He and I walked hand in hand, exploring their intricacies. This lasted about six or seven years, as far as I could tell, during which time I heard people crying, saw a lot of strange lights, listened to some policemen talk about me, and felt someone taking off my clothes.

I came to in the hospital. "What fresh hell is this?" I mumbled.

How long had I been gone? How many months? Years?

What strange new world had I awoken to?

And what of my family and friends? They must be worried sick!

I struggled to speak: "Nurse," I rasped weakly, "nurse, please, I need to tell everyone I'M OK! I'M ALIVE!"

She looked at me like I was some pathetic psycho strapped to a bed—which I was.

But what if everyone has moved or changed phone numbers? What if I don't have a home anymore? What if . . .

MICHAEL!

Of course, I'll call Michael! Michael would never change his number. He's solid. Reliable. The Rock of Gibraltar. Yes, I'll call Michael and he will be so relieved . . .

The nurse relented and dialed the number for me. I heard the familiar voice on the answering machine. How comforting.

"Michael!" I sobbed, "I'm OK. I'm back! I'm at St. Vincent's and they say I'll be all right!" and I wept tears of relief, "I'm going to be just fine!"

Feeling much better, I ripped the IV from my arm and fell out of bed. There was blood spurting everywhere. I was chased by a squad of goons with restraining belts as I stumbled naked into the hallway, flowers falling from my hair and elf ears still attached. I was quite a sight, I can tell you that. The blood, the green hair, the bobbing penis, the ears . . . I gave the staff something to talk about for days.

When I finally made it to the lobby, I was greeted by a touching group of ex-boyfriends, ex-roommates, and one confused little Spanish boy I was supposedly still on a date with. That they were all riffling through my lunchbox and doing my drugs, bothered me not a whit. These people were there for me.

Not so Michael.

My so-called best friend.

Later I learned that upon hearing that I had OD'd and was in the hospital, he had rushed *as fast as he could* to Save the Robots, an after-hours club that we were working at the time.

"James is in the hospital, so I should get all his drink tickets," Michael gleefully screamed to the owner. "And you might as well give me his pay, too. He won't be earning it tonight."

Hmph.

Then!

The next day, on Michael's outgoing message, *was my sickbed message of hope from the hospital!* "Michael, it's me, James—and I'm ALIVE!"

For everyone to get a good laugh over.

Isn't that hysterical? Evil, evil boy . . .

AND IF THAT WASN'T BAD ENOUGH—

There was a dinner party that night at a club in a diner, and when the food arrived, Michael *jumped on top of the table and grabbed a plastic butter knife.*

"EVERYBODY, LOOK AT ME! I'M JAMES ST. JAMES," he

mocked. He held the knife to his wrist: "PAY ATTENTION TO ME OR I'LL TRY TO COMMIT SUICIDE AGAIN!"

And that got a big laugh.

Later, he turned to me and said: "That's what you get for doing drugs, you big loser."

Funny how the pendulum swings.

STORY NUMBER FIVE

"This is the AT&T operator, collect phone call from a Michael Skrinkle Skroddle. Will you accept the charges?"

"Grudgingly, Yes, operator, I will accept. But very grudgingly."

Click. "Halloa? Skrod?"

"Yes, dear."

"Ech. These doughnuts are stale."

"Where are you?"

"Jail ska-da-da."

(Sigh.) "What are you doing in jail ska-da-da?"

"Eating doughnuts. Watching cable. Quick, turn on channel eleven . . . Lucy in the vat of grapes!"

I listened as he held the receiver up to the television for a full five minutes.

"MICHAEL! MICHAEL! GET BACK ON THE PHONE!"

"Yeeeeees?"

"I mean, what did you do to land in jail? . . . And how is it that you're watching cable and eating cake?"

"I told them I have AIDS. And my lawyer got me a special room. With my own phone. Quick turn on *The Simpsons!*"

This was going nowhere.

"Oh, and Skrod? I hope you don't mind, but when they arrested me, I gave them your name and Social Security number."

"Oh no, Michael. I don't mind. It makes **MY** jailhouse experiences *that much more . . . exciting*. You see, this way, I'm always surprised to find out how much trouble I'm actually in, when I see all the warrants you've piled up for me. No, really. Thanks loads."

"Want to hear why you're here?"

"I hope I at least had fun."

"Oh, you did. Believe me."

He told me a wildly convoluted story about picking up a hustler at the Port Authority and then breaking into a stranger's apartment to have sex and urinate on the furniture. Then somehow, after the cops came and there was a crazy chase sequence that ended up at the Javits Center, Michael took a two-by-four and broke a window to get in. And then assaulted the chasing officer with it.

"OK—I count Solicitation, Breaking and Entering, Sodomy, Sex with a probable minor, Vandalization by way of Urination, Resisting Arrest, Willful destruction of public property, and Assaulting a police officer . . . Do I have any outstanding warrants?"

"Just broken probation for the time I was caught buying heroin during my last arraignment."

"I did *what?*"

"Oh, I never told you about that? It's really a very funny story. That's when the judge recognized me from *Dateline* and asked for my autograph . . . Oh look at Rhoda's scarf!"

"I know. Apparently Valerie Harper got all the different ways to tie them from her personal secretary. My favorite is the turban style with the big ball in front. Makes my nose look smaller."

"You really should have a nose job, James."

"Thanks. Listen, I gotta run. Lunch tomorrow?"

"Stop by the club."

"Bye, Skrink."
"Bye, Skrod."

STORY NUMBER SIX

For almost nine months in 1990, I wore a bloody wedding gown and glued flies to my face. Some say I was a bit touched that year, and to be sure, there was a slightly unbalanced look about me then. I just like to think I was being fashion forward.

Anyway, after wearing this stunning ensemble day in and day out, every night for close to a year, I got a phone call from Michael.

"Oh My God! I just had *THE MOST ORIGINAL IDEA EVER* for Disco 2000. *You are going to be so jealous that you didn't think of it first . . .*"

"What now, darling? A party for the color green?"

"I'm going to call it *BLOOD FEAST* and everyone is going to be covered in blood and lying around with their arms and legs cut off and the poster is going to be Jenny eating my brains . . . What do you think you can do? Can you come up with a look for it?"

(Sigh.)

"Gosh, Michael, I don't know. I've never thought of anything as creative as wearing a *FUCKING BLOODY FUCKING OUTFIT TO A GODDAMN NIGHTCLUB BEFORE!* You're right, boy, that is *SO FUCKING ORIGINAL I WISH THAT I'D FUCKING THOUGHT OF IT.*"

"Well, get to work on something. It's next Wednesday night."

And so it came to pass that I was strapped to a gurney and covered in raw liver and slabs of beef that very quickly turned rancid under the bright spotlights. There exists a videotape somewhere that documents me being wheeled about the dance floor by two burly "orderlies," while I desperately search for a bathroom big enough to accommodate the stretcher so I can do a bump of cocaine. Watching me retch from the decomposing meat, and simultaneously fiend for drugs, makes for an entertaining time, indeed.

When I told my mother the extremes I went to in order to make a living, she just shook her head and said, "Now don't you wish you'd finished college, dear?"

Mother's are so wise, sometimes.

STORY NUMBER SEVEN

A city of cardboard dwellings had sprung up around Michael's neighborhood.

We had to stop and gawk—some of them were really quite amazing.

"Oh, James! How fun!"

He knocked on the flap of a two-story dwelling.

"Woo-hoo? Anybody home?"

A funny little man with an abscessed nose came out. He gave us the grand tour of his stylish split-level home. It was a triumph of architectural ingenuity. There was a massive foyer that led into a sunken living room. Then there was a hallway that led into a spacious sleeping loft.

All made out of common, everyday grocery boxes!

Of course, the plumbing was less than adequate. It consisted mainly of some jars that he labeled and saved, and a hole in the back of a box. But, hey, if that's how he liked it, who am I to argue?

"OH! OH! OH! OH MY GOD! I HAVE THE BEST IDEA EVER!"

I could hardly wait for this one.

And it was a doozy.

We were going to rent the shanties from the homeless people and all the club kids would sleep in them for the whole night. It would be just like living in a little kid's play fort!

He ran home and had the club's publicist call Phil Donahue—"To film it all, of course." There's no sense doing something if you can't get a little publicity out of it.

"It's a perfect angle! The press will eat it up! 'THOSE WACKY CLUB KIDS HAVE DONE IT ALL! THEY ARE *SO JADED* THE ONLY WAY THEY CAN ENTERTAIN THEMSELVES IS TO LIVE LIKE HOMELESS PEOPLE!' "

I cringed. "As I recall, Michael, Marie Antoinette suffered a wicked backlash when she tried the same thing."

"Who's that? Who is she? A new club kid? Does Phil Donahue know about her?"

I threw my hands in the air.

Michael and several members of the Disco 2000 family DID end up camping out with the homeless and, reportedly, had a MARVELOUS time, although Donahue never did come to film it. I stayed home and felt smug.

Now, from that story I really felt his delusional lack of empathy, his determination that the world change to suit his views, and his need to have every move, every idea, validated by the press (remember: *It's only real if it makes it into print*).

But I'm philosophizing again.

Now let's get back to our story, already in progress.

THE MAVIS AND FREEZE CHRONICLES

Well, we certainly can't have a murder without Freeze. And you can't understand the larger story, unless you understand *his* story.

Freeze was three very different people, who lived, at various times, three completely different lives.

When I first became acquainted with him, he was a very talented and fiercely well-read young man. Rather quiet. He had a boyfriend for many years, a dog named Pickle, and a thriving hat business.

He was equally at home discussing Duchampsian ideology and *Melrose Place* plotlines. He could quote freely from Susan Sontag's "Notes on Camp," and most anything by Camille Paglia.

He had framed Schiaparelli prints hanging in his room, and he loved nothing more than to spend hours with me rhapsodizing over, say, Babe Paley's neck or the Duchess of Windsor's evolving hairstyles.

If I mentioned that I was *just a fool* for the decorative art nouveau ironwork I saw in Paris, he would look up from his sewing machine and murmur: "Oh, the subway station at Rue du Faubourg! Just divine! There are three books over there on the subject."

He was always dressed to the hilt, to the ABSOLUTE NINES, with a shock of bleached white hair; a menacing, Mephistophelian goatee; and any number of pierced and painted body parts. He made all his own clothes—marvelous little deconstructed pieces that were very much in demand.

So there he was, a witty little hat maker and dress designer, in a rather unenviable position: he was locked away in a bedroom at the home of Drag Terrorist Bella Bolski—forced into indentured servitude—running up saucy little frocks for Bella—sunrise, sunset—all day, every day, in exchange for room and board.

Now, that Bella, boy, she was a work of art . . . I really do need to digress here and tell you a little something about her.

He/she would wake up early every morning and bounce out of bed, humming a happy song. Then she'd skip to work, pausing only to hug bunny rabbits and kiss little babies. She was a happy-go-lucky girl, and her coworkers enjoyed her sparkling sense of humor. Yes, everybody loved the daytime version of Bella Bolski, the adorable imp.

But as the sun went down, and night began to fall, she underwent a mysterious transformation. Her brow furrowed. Her smile turned upside down. With each layer of foundation that she slathered upon her face, another layer of armor was bolted into place. By the time the world saw this towering diva, she was lurking in the dark corners of one of Peter's clubs, growling at the patrons. By the end of the evening, you could find her standing at the exit, like a looming gargoyle, barking, "Where the hell do you think you're going? You aren't going anywhere!"

And nobody dared. When Bella hosted a party, *SHE TOOK HER DUTIES SERIOUSLY.*

Why did she swing so maniacally from happiness to despair? Was her wig on too tight? Were her eyelashes too heavy? I contacted a prominent transvestite psychoanalyst on the matter, and Dr. Drag insisted Miss Bolski exhibited a definite case of borderline personality disorder. "Really." He emphasized, "IT'S NOT COCAINE. No siree, THAT'S NOT BELLA'S PROBLEM AT ALL. Bella doesn't touch the stuff. It's all in her head. NO COCAINE UP HER SCHNOZZ."

Well, that's what he said, anyway.

So. She had a regular sweatshop going in her apartment. Five or six lost souls, all working toward a common goal: the Beautification of Bella vis-à-vis that evening's outfit. There was Freeze on the sewing machine, her brother manning the wig station ("Bigger, I said! More volume, goddamnit!"), a faghag running errands and freshening drinks, and usually a random fan (terrified, really, poor thing) who's only job was to play "I'm Every Woman" by Whitney Houston *over and over and over again.*

All this, so that when she went out at night and sat in her dark corner, growling at the patrons, she looked flawless.

I loved the daytime Bella. And the nighttime monster was such a fascinating read, I couldn't put her down!

So that's how I knew Freeze. Toiling away at someone else's dreams. It was just like Rumpelstiltskin. Freeze was the fair maiden, forced to weave the impossible on a dusty old spinning wheel, while the evil old troll stomped about making demands.

He was a sad sort of creature. Funny, but remote. And you always wanted to hug him. Well, not exactly hug him—after all, he was a fussy old queen—but maybe touch his shoulder quickly as a gesture of sincerity and ask him: *What were HIS dreams? What were HIS goals?*

His dreams and goals were realized soon enough. *Picture it: 1994, the year of the club kids' last shout. Disco 2000 is on autopilot due to Michael's growing heroin habit. Everybody, it seems, is bored . . . restless . . . addicted. The time is ripe for a takeover. Can't you feel it? Clubland is looking for the Next Big Thrill.* That's when Freeze Number 2 came along. SuperFreeze. FrankenFreeze. The fulfillment and embodiment of all those pent-up frustrations he must have harbored while working in that back room.

It happened like this:

Typically, we would all end up back at Bella's after a night out—against our better judgment, *against our wills, actually.* We were held prisoner at Bella's every night for an after-hours "party."

Party?! Woo-hoo!

Well, I imagine kibitzing with a roomful of brain-damaged halibut would have been more fun than one of Bella's parties. It was always the same:

Nobody was allowed to talk. AT ALL. It made Bella tense.

Whitney told us how she was every woman several times.

And the cocaine supply dwindled until it was gone and we were fiending and tense, with full beards coming through our makeup.

But you couldn't leave. You weren't allowed. Days would pass. Popes would change, and still you would be huddled in that room—with Whitney reiterating time and again how *it's all in her.*

Am I making my case clear? These were NOT fun parties.

But there we were again. It was January 1994.

Freeze joined us, which was a welcome change, and he had two friends from Boston with him.

One of them was a palsied old lesbian named Mavis,* and honey, she was on a mission.

She wanted to UNDERSTAND the CLUB SCENE. REALLY GET TO THE BOTTOM OF IT. FIGURE IT OUT. BECAUSE THAT'S WHO SHE WAS. "I'M MAVIS. GOOD TO MEET YOU! I'M A PROBLEM SOLVER. IT'S WHAT I DO. AND I WANT TO UNDERSTAND THIS CLUB KID THING. DO YOU KNOW ANYTHING ABOUT THESE 'CLUB KIDS' "?

Well, bells went off, lights were flashing, and a hail of confetti rained down on her. This was her lucky day.

"Darling! Hello! You must sit right here, next to me, be-

---

*Over thirty if she was a day.

cause *do I have some stories for you!* I'm James St. James. I'm a Clarifier, that's what *I* do. It all began in third grade when my teacher said to me, 'Jimmy,' she said, 'you're really going places'—oh, wait, will you get me a line first, dear, we're going to be here a while . . . we're out? Already? WHY WE'VE ONLY BEEN TRAPPED IN THIS AIRLESS COFFIN FOR THREE DAYS! Oh dear . . . What . . . shall . . . we . . . do . . . ? Hmmmm. Oh, I've got an idea! Mavis, would you be a dear and run to the *bodega* on the corner and get one? two? no three bags, I think, of their finest cocaine? Anyway, so there I was—me and Bianca in the bathroom at BAM—oh dear, no. One of those fiends must have stolen all my money. NEVER TRUST A DRAG QUEEN! But, I will gladly pay you Tuesday for a bag of cocaine today. Anyway, I was telling you about my first time on *Oprah* . . ."

Days later, when Bella finally granted us all parole, Mavis and I had truly bonded.

She was a strange bird, to be sure—but, listen to this—what a plan!—*you know me:* always thinking, my brain never sleeps, so try this one on for size:

We came up with a wonderful Life Plan for Mavis. She was going to invest all her life's savings in a bunch of cocaine. She would quit the job she loved—managing a health food store in Boston—sell her house, move to New York, AND SHE AND FREEZE WOULD BECOME DRUG DEALERS!

I would show them the ropes, of course, and introduce them around and get them on guest lists—that sort of thing.

Sometimes I rent myself out as an Image Enhancer. Lucrative side gig.

"Baby, I can make you both stars!" That's how I put it. And they were sold. "You two are going to be, *hold on to your hats,* CLUB KID DRUG DEALERS! Oh, you'll make a fortune. They all do. AND FUN! *Woo Doggie!* You'll have the time of your lives. You'll look back on it for the rest of your lives!"

Here Mavis interjected. Very seriously, she took my hand, looked into my eyes, and said: "I'VE GOT A REALLY GOOD FEELING ABOUT THIS. THIS IS WHAT I'VE ALWAYS DREAMED OF. AND NOTHING WILL GO WRONG, BECAUSE *I'M A BUSI-NESSPERSON. THAT'S WHAT I DO. I KNOW NUMBERS AND MARKETING.* That's what's missing in the club scene: A TO-GETHER, ORGANIZED, BUSINESS-SAVVY DRUG DEALER."

Pause.

Really let that sink in. Because I am going to hammer home the irony here. *Oh, I wish we could cut to sometime next year. It's delicious. It's hysterical. But no.*

Anyway.

I looked at Freeze. Visions of happy drug addicts danced in his eyes as he contemplated WHAT **HE** WAS GOING TO WEAR when his clients, *no, make that **his fans,*** came to *him* for a bump of cocaine.

"Yes. Hmmm. Good idea."

Of course, I was just chattering like a magpie. I was all loopy from lack of sleep. I didn't even know what I was saying. *I certainly didn't expect her to actually go through with it . . .*

PARTY MONSTER

But about, oh, a month or so later, there she was in her new New York apartment and she turned to me and said:

"Should I wear the polka-dot spandex dress or this tailored suit with the big shoulder pads to *really let them know I mean business*—I mean, this is my debut. I have to look just right . . ."

"Oh, the shoulder pads. Definitely the shoulder pads. They'll *love* them at Limelight. Trust me."

She had taken thirteen thousand dollars out of the bank. Her life savings. Ten years of work. Her rainy-day fund.

"No more rainy days for you! From here on in it's Sunshine and Lollipops!"

There was more coke than we knew what to do with. Enough to keep Bella quiet for . . . weeks. And Special K . . . and Rohypnol for when you want to come down . . . and Valium for when you get cranky . . . and heroin for Freeze . . . And what else? A little GHB. Some pot.

Then I turned to her and clutched her shaky little hand: "I have a good idea. You should let *me* carry the drugs around. I'm a star, the guards won't touch me. Of course, you trust me, right?"

"Oh sure. Of course. My God—JAMES, I CAN FEEL IT— YOU AND I ARE SO MUCH ALIKE. I FEEL LIKE I FOUND A BROTHER!"

I looked at this funny old coke freak with her spiky lesbian hair and her big watery eyes that looked so eager and happy, and I thought, "Oh well. I guess I can do this."

So, out of the goodness of my heart, because I am a good person, really, I decided that we WOULD be two peas in a pod, if that's what she wanted. And, by God, I was going to show her the time of her dreary little life.

These would be the best three months she will ever experience.

Because that's what I gave it. Three months. Then crash and burn. We had already done fifteen or so grams to celebrate the opening of our joint business adventure.

"LOSS LEADER," she rationalized.

"Oh, and Mavis, will you front me a bit for tonight? I'll call my accountant in the morning and she'll wire the money. I'm good for it. I'm James St. James."

"WHATEVER YOU WANT HONEY. AND TAKE AN EXTRA GRAM ON ME."

She went to the safe and extracted the goods.

"BUT WAIT FOR MAMA. I'M GOING TO MATCH YOU BUMP FOR BUMP. LINE FOR LINE. WE'RE IN THIS TO-GETHER."

Oh, greater men than you have tried and failed to keep up with me, honey! But, hmmm . . . something tells me . . . yes . . . you just might have it in you. Yes, I see the love in your face, it shows when it's gliding up the nose.

I looked at her again, in a new light.

"Mavis, you just might discover a whole new side of yourself. I think this will be a voyage of self-discovery for you."

She hugged me tight—"Oh, I hope so."

Freeze was in the next room, moussing his new sideburns. They were razor sharp—RAR!—and he dyed his hair FIRE ENGINE RED.

Now if he can just . . . get . . . the eyebrows . . . exactly right . . .

Not faggy, you see. But arched, *like this.*

And it will only take another hour to pencil in this goatee.

As I left the room, I heard him humming "Rose's Turn" from *Gypsy:*

> *Gangway world, get off of my runway, . . .*
> *This time boys, I'm taking the bows!*

Oh, I think we were all going to learn a lot about each other in the coming months.

And so we went out—each of us soaring miles above the earth, lifted by the drugs—but buoyed by the *realization of all our hopes and dreams.*

Mavis was going to be popular! famous! loved! And applauded for her business skills!

Freeze was going to be in the center from now on. No more backseat living for him! He was about to explode.

And me . . . well, I had a new sister . . . who cared a GREAT DEAL FOR ME . . . a sister with thirteen thousand dollars of fun in MY pocket.

Of course, it all went off beautifully, as planned.

The kids at Limelight *really did love her*—"Where on earth did you find this one, James?" they all asked.

"She was working at a grocery store in Boston. Isn't that fabulous?"

"GENIUS!"

At one point, a pink-haired nobody leaned over to her: "Mavis, I just worship your outfit. Those shoulder pads are so *retro-aggro-chic!*"

"Very butch, Miss Thing," somebody else chimed in.

Mavis tittered. Flattered that these *club kids* would actually acknowledge her! Little Mavis, who this time last month was an aging spinster . . .

But let's not dwell on the past.

It's all about RIGHT NOW.

"Oh, and right now, I think you ought to give Loretta Hogg—the drag queen over there with the pig snout—SHE'S VERY FAMOUS—I think you ought to give her a gram."

"Oh. Right. Right. Loretta Hogg. Remember that: very famous. Deserves a gram. Of course she does. Whatever you say. I trust you."

"Oh, and over there—that drag queen?—she's very famous too. The one with the four arms and the walrus tusks. A LEGENDARY LEGEND. Never pays for drugs . . ."

"But, wait . . ."

"LOSS LEADERS, MAVIS. Don't you know anything? Keep the stars happy and everyone else will follow. That's the rule. Always keep the people on top happy and you co-opt their fabulousness through association. You'll see."

"OK."

"And I'll need another gram to get through this. *She's such a bore!*"

"I thought she was famous . . . A legendary legend?"

I threw my arms up in disgust.

"Looks like we're going to have to break out the old flash cards. Remedial Nightclubbing 101, Spring session! OK, very slowly . . . yes, she's fabulous, Mavis, but that doesn't make her an interesting person."

"A green transvestite with four arms and walrus tusks isn't interesting?"

"Maybe at your *little granola factory* that passes for interesting. But this is the tippy-top, Mavis. You're at the *red-hot center* of the coolest club in the world. You can't get any higher than this, baby."

Was I laying it on too thick? What would she say when she learned the truth?—that even the most fabulous club kid is still rated somewhere between Don Knotts and Regis Philbin on the register of international hip.

"Truth is, Mavis, most of the people at the top are real nightmares. Monsters. Not worthy of you at all. They aren't real people like you and me. They've been corrupted. Why there's one, his name is Michael Alig—well, you stay away from him. Trust me on this one; he will take advantage of you, Mavis. And I'm only telling you this because I love you. But Michael will try to lure you away from me—he'll tell you lies about me, I know he will—*just to cause trouble.* He does that every day before breakfast. Every day he wakes up and says 'How can I cause trouble for James?' He's evil. Pure Evil."

Intuitively, he was right there. By my side. His antennae were tingling. He knew something was up.

"Why, Michael, I was just talking about you!"

"Of course you were, James. What *else* do you ever talk about? Hmmm. Who's your interesting new friend here?"

I pretended to find a fascinating new way to fold cocktail napkins.

La La La.

"Well, if James is going to be SO RUDE—Hi. I'm Michael Alig. Welcome to my club."

Mavis's mouth dropped.

"OK! OK! OK!" I screamed, "Michael this is Mavis. Mavis this is Michael. Yea. Yea. Yea. He is the king of all we survey. But, Michael, Mavis picked *corn* for a *deli* in Massachusetts. She's my new superstar. Oh. And she's also a drug dealer."

"AHA! I understand perfectly." And he shot me a look which said that he . . . understood. . . . Perfectly.

"Now, Mavis, don't you listen to a word James says. He's a bitter old has-been. He has no power here. Take it from me . . ."

And he threw a few dozen drink tickets at her and escorted her to the bar.

"I'm the one you should be talking to. It's all about me. James *used to be someone* . . . When were you famous, James? The fifties?"

I could see the wheels spinning. They were shooting off sparks, they were going so fast.

"You know you're absolutely wonderful," he continued. "We're going to get along like two peas in a pod. Yes. You know I have this little magazine, *Project X*, have you heard about it?"

Mavis suffered a mild stroke, which pleased Michael to no end.

"You would be perfect for a feature we're doing on the new 'IT GIRLS.' Of course, we'd have to set up a photo shoot for next week . . ."

I couldn't take it anymore.

"GODDAMNIT, JUST GIVE HIM A VIAL OF COKE AND A VIAL OF K—Michael, it's been wonderful spending time with you. It always is. But, look! Oh My God! Isn't that Michael Musto over there? He looks thirsty. Maybe *he'll finally be your friend* if you go talk to him right now."

"Don't think I don't see right through you, James St. James." And he took his drugs and scampered off.

I took Mavis into a stall.

"You are in league with the devil, woman. I'm telling you the truth. Yes, Michael can be dazzling. But it's just surface shine, dear. He doesn't have a soul. Or a heart. Please don't trust him, whatever you do. Yes, he can do a few things for you. BUT YE GODS, at what price? He will bleed you dry and toss your withered corpse aside. He's done it before."

I shook her violently, trying to impart the urgency of my message.

"I know you need to make money—but *is that really what you're all about?* I thought this was about helping each other, being there for each other, A SPIRITUAL JOURNEY, MAVIS, that we make together. It's about FAMILY. Weren't we all going to get an apartment together? Michael isn't one of us. He's a scheming, manipulative monster—only out for himself. You shouldn't even talk to him."

"DON'T WORRY," said a suddenly confident Mavis, "I CAN HANDLE MICHAEL ALIG. But he is a fascinating case study. I want to talk to him. Get inside his head. He's a businessman. I can tell. Just like me. I bet if we put our heads together. . . . But don't worry. He can't pull anything over on me. I'M SMARTER THAN MICHAEL ALIG. I WAS THIRD IN MY CLASS AT BOSTON UNIVERSITY. HE'LL NEVER CON ME."

Please.

PLEASE!

PLEASE LET ME SKIP AHEAD A YEAR. Just six months! You'll love it. Of course, you already know that no good can come of any of this. So please, let me just show you a quick picture—

Thanksgiving, maybe—when Mavis and Michael are thrown out of Tavern On The Green for smoking crack under the table . . .

Oh. OK. But just you wait.

We'll put the Mavis saga on pause there, and rejoin Freeze in the chapel of the Limelight. The dead center of the chapel to be precise. Surrounded by a large group of clubgoers **hanging on his every word.**

Freeze was delighted to discover how amusing he was—how everybody, suddenly *got* his eclectic brand of humor. The witticisms fairly tripped off his tongue and were greeted with gales of laughter from charmed freaks everywhere.

He was the life of the party—his sideburns were a hit! Why on earth had he languished at Bella's beck and call all those years? Why wasn't he here all that time, with people who appreciated him for who he was?

The man beneath the chaps. The real Freeze. These earnest and caring drag queens *saw the real him.*

He, too, had given away and consumed most of his drugs. Passing out bumps to the little people was *such fun.* And he used the drug-filled straw— with *your* bump on it—as a pointer, to stab and drive home the punch lines to his fascinating stories, so that in order to do your bump *you had to listen to the whole story and chase the straw around with your nose for half an hour.*

Freeze just babbled on while your bump hovered just out of reach, always one step ahead of your nose . . .

If you didn't know that's what was happening, it was a very funny sight to walk in on, indeed. Freeze in the middle of a crowd, surrounded by what looked like a dozen little kangaroos bobbing their heads in unison. Bobbing and weaving, chasing the straw.

Yes, Freeze was quite a mess that night. I'm not sure whether or not he knew what he was doing then. Torturing people by withholding their bumps.

But soon enough it would take on a sadistic quality. He learned the art of making people dance for their dinner, seeing how long he could make them suffer, while he looked more and more fucked up. That way, you could never say: "Freeze, you're fucking with me" because being a mess means it's never your fault.

You're the crazy one.

"James, you're paranoid. Of course you can have a bump. I'm giving it to you right now. GOD. YOU ARE SO IMPATIENT. I'm just feeling my X."

It was an infuriating game.

But Bella had probably been doing it to him for years.

"Let him have his moment."

That became my mantra in the coming months.

There was a party afterward, at Mavis's new place. A rip-roaring wingding, as far removed from anything at Bella's as we could get. And it was filled with Very Important Drag Queens. Movers

and Shakers. Tippy-top, each and every last one of them. Not a hanger-on in the bunch. No sir.

So of course there was a blizzard, a never-ending, complimentary blizzard for your nasal enjoyment.

I saw Mavis get tense near the end, when the abacus in her head started adding it all up.

She and Freeze retreated to the bedroom to count up the night's grosses.

She had her little ledger and her little Cross pen. This was all going to be accounted for. This was all going to be legit. She went to college for this.

Hmmm . . .
The night's profits . . .
Why, it says here . . . ?
That can't be right! . . .
I don't understand.
It says here, we LOST $2,000!
How did that happen?

"I owe you seventy-five dollars," I offered, "and we did that bump in the stall . . ."

"NO. NO. NO. IT'S NOT YOU, JAMES. I trust you. But somehow we're in the hole."

We all stared at each other blankly, uncomprehending. That's strange. I remember lots of transactions. I saw her hand out, why, *dozens of vials and bags!*

"It must have been Michael," I concluded, "I told you not to trust him."

"No that's not it. I think we just gave too much away."

"*Gurgle snerf,*" Freeze said in agreement (although between you and me, giving away too much was never Freeze's problem in those days).

"Well, yes and no," little old helpful me put in his two cents. "Now, Mavis, it was your first night. Of course, you had to make a splash. Now everyone knows you. They like you. They saw how generous you are. And more importantly, THEY SAMPLED YOUR WARES. They know now that they're dealing with quality. You HAVE TO GIVE A LOT AWAY in the beginning, to spread the word, to build a name . . . to build a solid reputation . . . for *good drugs dealt to you with a smile*. Service with a smile."

Oh ha ha ha ha.

(You see that's actually a very clever pun. Pause here to let it register. "Services" is drag slang for cocaine, as in: "I need some services here, Miss Thing!" So: *Services with a smile*. They should make T-shirts! *I am so good* . . .)

"You're right" she agreed, "You are always so right. Establish ourselves. Let everybody sample it so they know how really good this shit is . . ."

"And it **is** good shit, Mavis."

"Yea."

"Really good shit."

"Uh huh."

"That's some amazing shit."

"Do you want a line?"

"I'd love one—you're a doll."

Freeze had passed out on the couch, upside down and contorted like a pretzel.

Mavis and I did some more coke and I congratulated her on a marvelous debut, and then we had a

really

long

talk

about the importance of balancing your checkbook. Then after two or three hours, it veered into something about "prioritizing invoices"—I couldn't quite follow—she was clearly excited by it, though. She was screaming and leaping about the room, digging through drawers, drawing me "diagrams" that were incredibly detailed and accurate squiggle lines that missed the page entirely and were written on Freeze's silk pirate shirt.

"*Whoops!*" she laughed. We both laughed.

"Special K must be kicking in. Motor skills—GONE!"

Hmmm. I may have met my match in this one.

Imagine, I meet a crop duster from Ohio, and she can keep up with James St. James. Bump for bump.

She was good.

Now if we could just get her to stop shaking like that, and get her off the floor. "No, Mavis, you didn't lose a gram!"

Or did you?

Maybe I should check.

Just to be safe.

So we crawled around and picked at the carpet, until suddenly it was night and it was already time to start getting ready.

How did that happen?

The whole day just slipped away like so many bags of cocaine.

Freeze needed a solid three hours to get ready, and when we woke him up he leapt off the couch and ran to the sewing machine.

"I was just having the most marvelous dream. All about fluorescent armbands . . ."

"Oh goodness. Yes. It's *all about* the fluorescent armbands for spring. Absolutely."

What in the HELL was a fluorescent armband?

That's ridiculous!

"Get me a light!" he pointed to his lighter, sitting right next to him. There was an odd, imperious tone to his voice—one I had never heard before.

"Of course, darling."

Well, it turns out, in case you haven't guessed: fluorescent armbands are . . . bands . . . that go around your arms . . . around your biceps . . .

And they're fluorescent . . .

Always on the cutting edge, that Freezer.

He put on a completely different pair of identical chaps . . . moussed, THEN GELLED his sideburns this time . . . penciled in his goatee, then BLENDED each line . . .

A trademark look was forming here . . .

Superhero Leather Fag.

He spent four hours getting ready, and he looked exactly the same as when he woke up.

Drug addicts are so funny that way. Just spinning around, lost in their own little world. Doing so much, accomplishing so little.

How sad.

But, we'll think about that later. Right now, I needed another bump, and then I was teaching Mavis all about the history of the ficus.

A funny thing happened that night when we went out. When we got to the door of Club USA, the doorman, the toughest in New York, said: "You must be Myrtle. I mean Mavis. You canned tomatoes in New Mexico, didn't you? And now you're the new IT Girl." He looked her up and down. "That's a witty interpretation of spandex—go right in."

Who'd have thunk it?

And there were many joyful reunions for Freeze. All night long, he found REALLY GOOD FRIENDS, and once again he was at the top of his game—the new Tallulah Bankhead! And I mean that literally. Tossing off the bons mots, while face down in the toilet. Now that I think about it, he even sounded like her: smug, imperious, pampered, slurred.

Mavis, too, made quite a splash. She was enthralled by the freak show and wanted to REALLY GET TO KNOW each and every little cowboy and fairy princess that traipsed past.

And the freaks responded to her, in kind. They looked at her like she was, well, *let's call a spade a spade*—like she was a grocery bagger from the A&P in Minnesota.

Which she was.

So she gaped at them and they gaped at her. She was the oddest thing they'd ever seen. That hair! Was she serious?

But one thing I'll say on the club kids' behalf—they are nothing if not open-minded. And Mavis was so drop-dead normal looking, she could have been from Mars.

And, again, who'd have figured? I was right! By keeping the "superstars" happy with free drugs, they managed to become rather high-profile themselves. It got to the point where no party could start without them. They were as indispensable as drink tickets and disco balls.

And grasshopper Freeze had learned well the Lessons of Divadom from Bella.

His entrances became precisely and dramatically timed.

He learned that for every party there is *that one glorious moment*—when all the right people have arrived and found their optimum posing space . . . and they are saying all the right things . . . and the energy level rises . . . and the glamour and the excitement bubble up into a frothy, heady, undeniable crescendo of chic.

When it's right, you can feel it from the tip of your heel to the top of your wig.

Freeze discovered the trick of arriving *just scant moments AFTER the peak SHOULD HAVE OCCURRED*, but somehow fizzled . . . and then, while everybody *wants* to scratch their heads in confusion (but just can't muss that 'do), and while they look around in disappointment to see what went wrong . . . Suddenly

KAPOW!

The Dynamic Duo breeze into the room, wearing their space-age headphones (*de rigueur* for the modern drug-dealing team), and there is a great whoop of joy—"Oh! THAT'S what was missing!"

Mavis and Freeze!

"Let the festivities begin!"

They gave away lots.

And consumed copious amounts themselves.

So they simultaneously lost much money through their hobnobbing with the hoi polloi, and, in so doing, they earned a loyal legion of wanna-bes who more than compensated. They paid cash to be included in all the fun.

So they then started making money—an inordinate amount of money, a sinful amount of money.

And when the money keeps coming in, when the geyser is gushing, who can count each and every droplet? It would be petty to do so.

"Can I borrow these boots, Freeze, dear?" I asked one starry night.

"Only if I'm not wearing my chaps, dear."

I put them on anyway, and in the toe was a wad of three thousand dollars.

"Well, hello!"

"I'll be damned."

"Where'd that come from?"

We were forever finding wads and eightballs and little expensive things they had just plum forgotten about. It made getting dressed *so much more interesting*... every outfit was a little Cracker Jack box just waiting to be opened and mined for fun.

And just look at them! Why, they even look different! Success and money and power can do marvelous things!

They say that God is in the details, and FREEZE WAS GOD at this point.

He began using bronzer, ALL OVER, a two-hour applica-
tion requiring multiple blending drones—whoever was at hand:
"Could you please, in that bowl over there, stir together two-
thirds Estée Lauder Super Tan with one-fifth Dior Instant Glow,
chill, then add four spritzes of Hawaiian Tropic? Now, at twenty-
minute intervals, apply and blend *(evenly, now)* from the forearm
to the wrist. Three times." This is repeated on **each body seg-
ment,** until EVERY INCH has that marvelous Chef Boyardee
glow that we all covet.

And Mavis, with her new stylish shag, is no longer content
wearing dreary old power suits. She has perfected the age old:
"Oh NO! Pat's closes in ten minutes! Quick, tell the salesgirl I
need two silver somethings, and damn the expense!"
That way, later on, when a compliment comes your way,
you can languidly acknowledge it *like so:*
"Oh *this?* You really like it? I only had *ten minutes* to
throw it together! Can you believe? But I guess it does work,
hmmm?"
That's class.

Weeks passed quickly.
We went out every night—dressed to the teeth. Or
dressed to the dentures in Mavis's case. Bless her heart.
I've got to hand it to her though, she was a quick learner.
And as Pop Art Drug Dealers, they looked fabulous while
providing an invaluable service. People loved them.
And from there it only got bigger. A feeding frenzy hit
clubland; Mavis and Freeze fever!
Mavis dyed her hair purple!
Crazy Mav!

(But strangely, on her, it just looked . . . normal. Style seemed to just slip off her.)

So they were "IT."

Worshipped. Adored.

Crowds followed them.

Boys threw themselves at Freeze, girls at Mavis. Both were ecstatic. Why hadn't they even noticed their stunning sexual appeal before?

Bella was furious that Freeze and I had become so close. And that he had unofficially moved into Mavis's.

I was spending most of my time there, too.

My tab was rising, I owed them almost five thousand dollars, but didn't give it a second thought—we were having such fun. We did so much cocaine, *asteroids were falling out of our noses.*

It turns out Mavis was an endlessly fascinating woman. We spent days exploring the intricacies of each other's minds.

I don't remember drawing any conclusions, though.

But I have dozens of pie charts that explain it all, if you care to look.

It all seemed so deeply profound and urgent at the time. Oh well.

Freeze would get so disgusted with us.

He would pass out for fourteen or fifteen hours at a time. When he woke up and came into the living room, Mavis and I would still be having the EXACT SAME CONVERSATION AS WHEN HE LEFT. Word for word.

"I just LOVE Oreos . . ."

"Oh. Oreos. Yes. But not DoubleStuf . . ."

"Well, it's just too much *filling*, don't you think?"

"Definitely. But now the original . . . Oreos . . . are just wonderful."

"Yes. I love a good Oreo now and again."

FOR HOURS! Until Freeze would just start throwing things.

What he didn't understand though, was it was all about **THE SUBTEXT** of those conversations. The subtext spoke volumes.

Usually on the third consecutive day of massive drug consumption and no sleep, I hit my stride.

That's when I LOOKED MY BEST—like a slightly crazed supermodel.

And I was shockingly articulate . . .

AND FUNNY!

I had them rolling in the aisles at the Limelight!

Peeing their pants at Robots!

Like the time I took the vacuum cleaner to the club—because "it looked dusty"—and pretended to be the cleaning woman! . . .

Sheer hilarity!

"That Michael sure makes me work for my hosting fee!" I told everyone on my coffee break. Then I start vacuuming again.

Sometimes I'd ride a broomstick around all night, or spontaneously go-go in my jockstrap.

And when I played "Nearer My God to Thee" on a dozen beer bottles—well, I brought down the house.

Now on the fourth day, things can start getting a little dicey.

Emotions are running high—who knew there were so many reasons to just start sobbing? And You and Rational Thought parted ways some time ago—probably *before* the three peyote buttons, but definitely *after* you sucked off the crack dealer on the corner.

Yes, the fourth day is tricky. Let me warn you: there are traps and pitfalls along the way. Like when you decide that it's finally time to have that heart to heart with your roommate and discuss all the things you dislike about him.

Hold off on it. Don't do it.

Day Four is full of red herrings to trip you up. It *sounds* like a good idea. Of course, honesty is the best policy, and communication is *so* important, and I know that toothpaste thing *really* bothers you, but—

TRUST ME ON THIS ONE:

Day Four is not the time to have that conversation.

In fact, any conversation is fraught with potential danger. Lurking behind every syllable could be a double meaning—*"Just what EXACTLY did you mean when you said it looked like it might rain? Are you reverting to cliché to comment on my supposed 'lack of insight'? Is this really about that boy I slept with three years ago?"*

Many people get into very violent fights over very trivial things on this day. Watch yourself. You may be more irrational than you think.

Sometimes Day Four is the perfect time to clean your closet. Again, trust me. I know it looks dull. But once you get into it, it will become an all-encompassing, never-ending Sisyphean task. But, it's a feel-good trip down memory lane, and *you will cry* when you find that little pink miniskirt that makes you look just like Belinda Carlisle (A SKINNY BELINDA! A SKINNY BELINDA! I didn't mean anything by that!).

And if maybe you just happen to crawl inside the closet and shut the door and wait for the bad things to go away . . . ?

WELL GOOD FOR YOU. That's the most sensible idea you've had since Tuesday when you cut out all those pictures of Linda Evangelista and glued them to your wall in a swirly pattern. You'll never regret that move, no siree.

I believe it was on a fourth or fifth day of unbridled depravity that we fell so low, even I am ashamed of my actions.

We had long since passed the point of mindless chatter. *That was days ago*—when we still liked each other, and we could still combine *vowels* and *consonants* to form WORDS. By now, we had taken to clattering quietly, each in our own corner—Jennytalia, Mavis, and me—watching the dust bunnies, between each carefully doled out bumplet of cocaine. I mean, we subsided on whiffs of hints of lint. *And you had better really NEED that granule of lint*—you had better have a doctor's note saying it was a medical emergency, a matter of life and death . . . because it was almost gone, and Mavis was feeling a bit persnickety.

We all looked like hell. Both Mavis and I had that "gravy skin face." And Jenny was stunning, as usual, but an odd shade of *greige*.

I know, I know—we should have stopped all this madcap hilarity a few days ago, when everyone we've ever known left us in disgust. They called us "gross" and "greedy." But like ants and rubbertree plants, we had high hopes and determination coming out of our ears. Uh, noses. *We were going to ride this one out! Never say die! It's not over till it's over!*

And it was almost over.

Occasionally, I tried for a bit of levity, but my performance of "I'm a Little Teapot" was met with stony, irritated glares. This I interpreted as peevishly withheld applause. At any other time, my wildly inventive "spout" usually rates at least a gush, or a deep, scraping bow of respect.

Jenny did what Jenny does after days of drug taking: she got on the floor and began searching for long-lost bits or bags of cocaine.

Normally, we would lift her up by the scruff of her neck and tell her to . . . just . . . stop it.

But, hey, maybe she was on to something this time. Maybe there really WAS a long-lost gram between the cushions, or behind the bookshelf. It happened all the time!

Suddenly, Jenny wasn't so crazy after all.

In fact, *now that you mention it,* we all remembered putting a stash aside for emergencies. But was that yesterday? Or last month?

Our search became more frantic as we convinced ourselves that there WAS INDEED a treasure trove of cocaine somewhere, somewhere within our reach.

We searched the furniture—in fact we dismantled it and ripped open the upholstery. Then *we stacked every piece in the corner of the room.*

We systematically covered EVERY INCH of that apartment, and with each passing hour, we only grew more hell-bent on finding the now-legendary eightball.

We drained the waterbed, and inspected it underneath and inside.

We ripped the linings out of jackets.

We checked each ice cube for a frozen treat in its center.

We emptied cereal boxes, went through the neighbors' trash, and even strip-searched *each other*—"I never trusted either one of you!"

Just as Mavis was about to get under the sink, dismantle the pipes, and begin roto-rooting—

Jenny became convinced that she distinctly remembered *it had dropped behind the radiator.*

Hmmm . . . yes . . . why, by cracky! I think she's right. In fact *I know* that's where it is.

"Yea! Yea!" agreed Mav. "It fell off the windowsill, *behind the radiator!* Of course!"

Jenny had the skinniest arm, so she tried first to reach down that narrow space between the radiator and the wall. The radiator was hot, and it burned her arm, severely, BUT NO MATTER, she . . . just . . . couldn't . . . quite reach.

"Get a wire hanger. Bend it like so."

She suffered a few more burns, but even the wire hook didn't work.

"I think I feel it though!"

Well . . . what if Mavis and I pulled at the radiator, really hard, and leaned it a bit more forward?

That could work.

So we sweated and huffed and wheezed and pulled with all our might . . . Our hands were hot, our faces were filthy, but, By God, we moved it an inch more out.

"There it is!" She made a stab at something, but—

"OH NO!"

There was a crack between the wall and the floor, behind the radiator, and she MIGHT HAVE PUSHED OUR SALVATION INTO THE WALLS!

There was only one thing to do:

Rip the radiator off the floor.

With a hammer, a screwdriver, and a crowbar—the three of us *CLEARED THAT OBSTACLE* out of the way. YES SIR! GOOD JOB!

I'm not making any of this up.

NOW: without that pesky old hot thing to slow us down, we could get on with our mission. All of us, flat-faced on the floor, with matches and later a penlight, peered into the crevice between the wall and floor.

"Why, Jenny, you're right."

That DID look like a Baggie.

Over there.

So we tried again, with the bad luck hanger—but, "Damn You, James!"—it only served to push *it* (whatever *it* was), underneath the floorboards.

YEP. YOU GUESSED IT.

With the trusty crowbar in hand, we began **tearing up the floorboards in Mavis's living room.**

We had taken off a good two or three rows—when Freeze walked in.

Picture this: the furniture was slashed and all neatly stacked in the western corner of the room. There was no bed. All food products had been emptied into one pile on the kitchen floor. Every piece of clothing was destroyed. The entire neighborhood's garbage was all right there, in the bedroom.

And there we were: sopping, stinking, blackened, and

crazed. Face down on a ripped-up floor. Next to an upside-down, nonfunctioning radiator.

"What in the hell is going on here?"
He wasn't angry, yet. Just baffled beyond belief.
We tried to play it down—*real casual-like*—we didn't want to look *desperate* . . .
"Oh, not much. How was *your* day?"

He wasn't biting.
Finally we had to tell him of our quest and its consequences.
I went to go get a beer to help calm him down. When—
On top of the refrigerator
I saw
a plate.

Not just any old plate. But a plate with an Everest-sized mountain of cocaine on it.
"Uh . . . guys?" I held it up.
"Oh yeah—I forgot all about that." Mavis said, as a matter of course . . . *just as blithe as Miss Danner herself.*

So we dug right in, and got all tense again, and didn't talk to each other for a number of days. Except to periodically look at one another with disgust and say: "I can't believe what a fiend you turned into there."

That was the spring of '94, a legendary binge that began in February and ended in July. I only weighed about twenty-seven pounds . . . But those were **SOME TWENTY-SEVEN POUNDS,** I tell you! Each and every one of them STYLISH TO A FAULT! TWENTY-SEVEN pounds of fabulosity!

I took a lot of acid that spring, as well, and throughout the month of April, I thought I was a space spider—*of course, of course*—and so I shaved off my eyebrows, pierced some things, dyed my hair green, then chopped bits and hunks of it off until there were four otherworldly antennae leaping from my head.

Because that's how space spiders styled themselves in 1994. And my patented Spider Dance never failed to slay them after hours.

Ah, youth! Such folly!

The nightly after-hours at Mavis's took on a quasi-mythical quality.

Every night Freeze and I dredged up a new "star" for Mavis to meet. We really did bring in a stellar mix. She got to meet some fascinating people, hard-to-meet people, A-listers.

And Mavis and I worked exceedingly well as a hostessing team.

We took turns, bouncing up and down, taking care of everybody's particular needs.

One of us would dazzle the crowd with witty banter and sophisticated anecdotes, and the other would, you know, make sure the ashtrays were emptied and there were enough free lines on the table.

We were a team! 50-50!

I really looked forward to these parties.

And the craziness at her house only intensified in the coming months. People came at all hours, in all conditions, and

144

stayed for days. They came alone, or with entire flotillas. There was an armless drag queen wearing a floral bikini who spent a great deal of time shivering behind Mavis's potted ferns. I remember one occasion when I suddenly realized that I'd spent two whole days describing my bloody stool to the Mexican delivery boy who didn't speak a word of English, but nevertheless, he had so much fun he quit his job and became a club kid.

Of course eventually things started getting dangerous, too much rickrack. And people started stealing, you know, little things like eightballs and boyfriends. And there were fights and mishaps. Ugliness was everywhere.

Then . . .

One day, Freeze accidentally sold a vial of K to a Latin King gang member who thought it was cocaine, and consequently this gang member fell into a K-hole.

A simple enough mistake. Happens quite frequently. I, personally, look forward to it. (K-holes, I mean.) But gang members are a notoriously humorless lot of people, and supposedly there was now a contract out on Freeze's life.

Now, really. A stern talking-to might have been in order. A bit of labeling advice, perhaps. But death? Because of a drug mix-up?

That's just silly. Things like that don't happen. Not in clubland.

Anyway.

On the night in question, Freeze was at my apartment packing up drugs for the evening. He did it there because the super at Mavis's building was getting suspicious of all the traffic in and out of her apartment.

Mavis and I were kickin' like chicken at her place, waiting

for the goodies to get back. The buzzer rang, and through the intercom an adorable dealer named Cookie-Puss said he was coming up, and it was "very serious business."

Now don't get me wrong. I love Cookie-Puss to death. I think the world of him. He's gorgeous. The face of an angel. Salt of the earth. Don't have a bad thing to say about him.

But I didn't have my face on. I looked a mite craggy. And I just didn't have the energy to compensate for a weather-beaten face by being witty. So I went into the bedroom. And pretended to be asleep.

Well, the door burst open, Mavis screamed, and all hell broke loose.

Cookie-Puss was not alone. Someone else was with him, and this someone pulled a gun on Mavis. "WHERE THE FUCK IS FREEZE? WHERE'S THE CASH? WHERE ARE THE DRUGS?"

Pickle, the dog, began barking loudly, and the gun was turned on Pickle. "SHUT THE DOG UP OR HE DIES TOO!"

Cookie-Puss, bless his heart, took Pickle into the bedroom, where I was pretending to be asleep.

"Oh, hi honey." I smiled and yawned, ignoring the hoo-ha in the other room, "How are you?"

"Oh, hi James. Sorry about this. Do me a favor: shut the fuck up. Shut the dog up. Don't come out of the fucking room and whatever you do, don't look at my friend. If he thinks you'll recognize him, he'll have to kill you."

"OK. But how are *you*?"

"Fine. Fine. Yourself?"

"Good."

"You *look* good."

"Thanks."

I heard crashing plates in the next room.

"WHERE THE FUCK IS FREEZE? THAT ASSHOLE IS

DEAD, DO YOU HEAR ME? WHEN WE FIND HIM, HE'S DEAD!"

Where the fuck was Freeze, indeed. He was due back twenty minutes ago. In fact he was probably on his way up the steps right now. That boy has the worst sense of timing... Wouldn't that be just like him to walk in right now?

The whole situation seemed more comical than deadly. Pickle and I giggled over Mavis's plight in the next room.

Cookie-Puss came back in the room and blew me a kiss.

"Sorry about this, James. See you later?"

"Don't worry about it, honey."

He smiled and I got hard. He stole the phone and warned us both not to leave the apartment or call for help or they'd come back and kill us.

I sat thinking about how sweet Cookie-Puss was for caring about me so much... I wondered if his friend was as cute as he was... How nice that he didn't want me to die... What a good husband Cookie-Puss would make... We could go around knocking off drug dealers together... I'd be his moll.

Mavis was slightly hysterical when I went to check on her. She was holding her neck. Apparently Cookie's hot little friend had tried to choke her and had played with her boobs, or something equally odd. I mean, who would play with Mavis's boobs?

"What did they take?"

"All they got were a few rolls of pennies and three grams of coke," she sobbed.

"Shit. I really wanted a bump of coke. You don't have *any?* I hope Freeze gets back soon."

Inexplicably, she threw a glass at me.

Post-traumatic stress, probably.

"FUCK YOU, JAMES!" she howled. "I WAS JUST FELT UP AT GUNPOINT, MY HOUSE WAS BROKEN INTO, BUT *LET'S*

WORRY ABOUT GETTING YOU A FUCKING BUMP! I AM SO SICK OF YOUR ATTITUDE, I COULD STRANGLE YOU!"

Then she ran to her bedroom to cry.

I think she'd been doing a lot of speed lately, too.

Freeze came home and seemed rather blasé about his death sentence. "What are ya gonna do?" He didn't think the Latin Kings were really after him. He figured Cookie-Puss got a little too sketched out on crack and concocted the whole story as an excuse to rob them.

Freeze must have been out of his mind, too. Would my sweetheart do something like that?

Daylight—Avenue C.

I ran into Cookie-Puss, lovely little Cookie-Puss.... He was looking a little haggard.

"J-J-James! H-h-how are you? W-w-want s-s-some c-c-coke?"

"No thank you. How are you, though?"

"G-g-great. Sorry about the other night. They really wanted to kill Freeze. I tri-tried to protect him, y'know. Th-th-that's why I was there. To protect him."

"Sure, honey. That was sweet. Maybe I will do just one bump."

We did it on the street corner.

"I'm going into rehab tomorrow," he said. "Six months."

"Good for you. I hope it works out."

We said goodbye. When I saw him three weeks later, he looked very bad indeed. Almost not cute. There were scabs on his face. Circles under his eyes. His clothes were dirty.

"Hi, Cookie-Puss," I said brightly. "My friend here needs some drugs. Can you help us out?"

"G-g-give me the money, quick. I'll g-g-get it for you."

My friend looked dubious.

"Don't worry," I assured him, "this is Cookie-Puss. A close friend of mine. Of course we can trust him!"

Cookie-Puss grabbed the money and ran.

"James, how do you know that person running off with my rent money?"

"Oh, he held me at gunpoint a few nights ago. Isn't he cute?"

Needless to say, I never saw Cookie-Puss again.

And I never again felt comfortable at Mavis's apartment, either. Her snippy manner, coupled with Freeze's increasingly imperial attitude, were wearing thin. They seemed to have forgotten all about my piquant charm, and the beguiling physical presence that drew them to me in the first place. In short, I started to feel like I was on the way out.

I knew it to be true when, one night, quite unexpectedly, Michael showed up at one of our after-after hours. Something he NEVER DID.

This was when Michael was still just dabbling in drugs, and exaggerating their effects. Going to a party at nine o'clock in the morning was inconceivable, back then.

But there he was. The mighty King of Clubs. At lowly little Miss Mavis's pad.

Both Mavis and Freeze were fluttering around him, fluffing

his pillows, refreshing his drinks. You would have thought he was the freakin' Queen Mother.

"No, no," he mock protested, "just treat me like you treat everybody else. Like I'm one of the group."

(Gag)

How dare he?

This was my territory and I bristled at the challenge his presence implied.

Now, usually Michael and I bounce off each other quite nicely—volleying back and forth at varying tempos, a few spikes here and there, the occasional slam.

There are certain stock stories we drag out on these occasions, stories that we believe enhance our images. Like the time I traded my car for a blowjob. Or the time Michael stole a city bus and had a party on it.

So it was in the beginning, but it soon became obvious that the stakes were much higher this time: it was an unspoken battle for the control of the room.

Back and forth it went, until all other conversations trailed off and everybody tuned in to this classic episode of *The Michael & James Show.*

We were neck and neck for hours, taking vicious potshots at each other, searing insults, blistering personal attacks . . .

He told everybody about my unruly shoulder hair. I countered with the story of how his butt fell inside out and he and Keoki had to push it back in with a pencil.

He talked about the time I chatted with DIANNE BRILL for twenty minutes with a giant snot bubble hanging from my nose.

"That's nothing compared to your little poop problem at Club USA."

"They have all sorts of wonderful acid peels now, James, that could get rid of that awful hamburger face of yours, honey, and then you wouldn't have to be embarrassed to be seen in the daylight."

And so on.

I could have held on. But just then, Bella, who still resented the fact that I wasn't spending any time with her and Whitney anymore, walked in and linked arms with Michael. He had an ally. I was doomed. Humiliated. They brought out pictures of my old tube skirt–and–fez phase. They giggled over my floating eye and body odor. They speculated on my impending spinsterhood, and worried about my palsy. I don't even remember the big finish, something to do with my wobbly eyeliner and lipstick on my teeth. I retreated to a corner in shame.

Michael won.

He showed he could not only keep up, but excel in this new milieu. He consumed *massive* quantities of drugs, the first time I'd ever seen him do so much and actually enjoy it. I felt sick to my stomach. I knew it was only a matter of time until he was Master of the Game.

I had lost serious ground. Michael had his foothold in Mavis and Freeze.

It can be rather disheartening to be best friends with a rattlesnake.

It's the little moments that are so telling:

Michael and I had been admiring each other in the mirror for about an hour.

Suddenly he turned to me and screamed: "OH! OH! I have *always* wanted to do this!"

He grabbed an electric razor and waved it menacingly in my direction.

"Skrinkle?" *Pause.* "Darling?" *Pause, eyes narrowed.* "Do you trust me?"

"No, not one iota."

"You don't trust me to give you the most FABULOUS hairdo of all time?"

"No, Michael, I do not trust you on a boat, I do not trust you on a goat. I do not trust you here. I do not trust you there. I do not trust you anywhere."

He was undeterred.

"My dear, you are going to look JUST GER-JIS! GRRRR-JIS," and, without warning, he rammed the razor upside my head.

"OW!"

"SHAVE AND A HAIRCUT—SKROD LOD!" He laughed and hit me again at another angle, taking off a very large hunk of head with it.

Interesting.

"The AIDS look!" he announced.

"Chemo Glam!"

"A few bruises here, some yellow around the eyes . . ."

"Flesh-Eating Bacteria!"

"Nicole Brown Simpson!"

"You look fabulous!"

I looked horrific.

He appraised my new look, then kept at it—hacking at me here, leaving a bloody gash there, right upside the old medulla oblongata-la-da-doo. Little hopeful sprouts stuck out at one side, and there was a sickly patch of fur left tufted on top.

"Oh, you look fabulous!" he said, without even looking. He had returned to admire his own thick mane. He smiled as he languorously combed his lush, unspoiled locks.

I can be **such a Clampett** sometimes.

I put on my dress, took off my shoes, and decided to go barefoot.

I was hardcore—RAR! What a look!

Of course, by the end of the night, my feet were the bloody carrier stumps of various staphylococcal infections from standing in the knee-high goo found in improvised bathroom stalls and walking on shards of glass on the dance floor . . .

Fake scabs on my face, real ones on my head and feet . . . Where did reality stop and image begin?

My sick new Sick Look was surprisingly real.

I scratched a scab on my head, and an ear fell off.

And then we were off. Twelve of us freaks piled into a limousine, on our way to one of those newfangled "raves" you've no doubt been hearing about. A rave is when thousands of blissed-out teenagers gather together in unsupervised, and often illegal, surroundings, like a field or an empty warehouse. Then they dance the night away to that heathen techno music, and celebrate the glory of peace, love, and baggy pants. This particular rave was being held at a high school in Poughkeepsie.

Let me just say: I don't believe Poughkeepsie was prepared.

It was still a two-hour drive, though. And that's a long time to be trapped in a car with Michael, Mavis, and Freeze.

"You know I've always thought that we should open a theme restaurant," Michael said, "and call it Café Auschwitz. Make it a big gray building with iron bars and barbed wire."

Everybody laughed.

"And only one course on the menu—water," added Freeze.

"Maybe a few finger sandwiches," I offered. "With real fingers!"

Mavis raised her hand excitedly: "Oh, and waif supermodels in deconstructed clothes fighting over lettuce leaves, looking emaciated and gorgeous!"

"And you could stamp numbers on customers' wrists when they come in."

"We could have really hot skinhead busboys in Nazi uniforms!"

"Oh My God! Let's do an ad for it in *Project X*. Get it to me by tomorrow morning."

And we were there.

We tumbled out of the car in what I thought was rather grand fashion—a cyber-clown fantasy—and rolled toward the entrance.

The doorman, a truly awful person nicknamed Peter-Peter Boyfriend Stealer, who just scant hours earlier had been one of my best friends, took one look at the group of us CLUB KIDS, and me in particular, and ran heading for the hills. He leapfrogged over the crowd, knocking over poor, dear, sweet Lady Miss Kier in his haste to dissociate himself from freaks like us. Whatever corner we turned, he vaulted over bars, disappearing into impenetrable areas of the school . . .

That's how embarrassing we were. Club kids were becoming *passé*.

My acid kicked in around then, and I got a little sad and paranoid.

I looked for a friendly face to reassure me. I saw Marlon, Keoki's new boyfriend, and hoped for the best. "Hey, Marlon!" I yelled and made a lunge for him.

"Nobody here likes you, James," he said, and ran the other direction.

Would you **ever** say something like that to someone on acid?

Well, thank goodness there were no great cliffs in Pough-keepsie, or I would have thrown myself off of one. And, fortunately for me, I suppose, Mavis and Freeze had just sold their last cyanide capsule.

I looked around for Michael, but he was rolling around on the floor with a new boy.

Daniel.

A sixteen-year-old boy named Daniel.

"Oh, James," he gushed when he surfaced. "This is the one. He really understands me. He's one of us!"

Daniel was wearing a leash and collar and Michael was walking him through the party on all fours. The boy was just adorable.

But as they were busy sucking face, I felt like a third wheel.

Next on my list of hopefuls was Mavis. But where was she?

She was having the time of her life when last I saw her— oh—and there she was now.

Mavis at a rave, well, that was a sight! "Ravin' Mav!" we called her, scootin' around the dance floor, like she had good sense.

The kids all did a double take when they saw her— "Granny at the Rave"— but she was surprisingly adept at picking up the lingo and sizing up the scene.

She'd flap her bony little arms like a chicken and blow her little jeweled whistle—nobody partied as hard as Mavis did! She would dance for days if we let her.

It was frustrating for me as her Spiritual Guide to just let her go. She was hopeless on her own; meeting all the wrong people, wasting her time on the dance floor. She should be in the back, schmoozing Lady Miss Kier, for God's sake—there was work to be done!

But look at her.

She's so happy. I bet this is the happiest she's ever been. Ever. In her whole life. I'm probably the best thing that's ever happened to her. Kier can wait. I noticed her edging into the shadows whenever I walked into the room. She probably had a zit or something and was embarrassed to see me.

But I was still all alone.

Gosh, it felt just *awful* to be unpopular!

I felt so awkward. What should I do with my hands? Should I sit, should I stand and dance in one place, keep moving?

I certainly didn't want to give off any "loser vibes," so I kept waving to nonexistent friends on the dance floor and mouthing *Be right there!* in the direction of the bar.

But then I heard:

"Girl? What are you doing?" and Freeze caught me. "There's nobody out there! Who were you waving at?"

"Oh, that isn't Michael? That looks just like Michael!" and I pointed to—quick, find someone—a fat black girl in the corner.

Whew! That was close!

"Girl, you need to slow down. As a friend, I'm just telling you. People are talking."

Again with that! Would you EVER say that to someone on acid? Some friends! Freeze's cruel streak was surfacing again. Better to just scream and run away sensibly than start a scene.

So Freeze, Marlon, and Peter were all against me. Michael found a new boy, we would not see him again for weeks. Mavis was useless and Lady Miss Kier had a zit and was hiding from me.

This was without a doubt the lowest, saddest moment of my life. Friendless in Poughkeepsie. Dancing alone on bloody stumps.

At least I looked amazing. I'll give me that much.

Whoops. There goes my other ear. Did I just lose my other ear? Well, at least searching the ground for a lost ear was a viable solution to standing there looking like a doofus.

This new boy of Michael's, Daniel, was soon a welcome addition to our little family. Delightfully subversive, willfully self-destructive, but with a pair of puppy dog eyes that you could happily fall into forever, he really was quite a charmer. Michael was sold on him by the end of the rave, when he started to cry at the thought of leaving Michael's side. He ran away into the city quite often to visit.

I'm all misty just thinking about it now.

I'll be honest.

I loved Daniel like I loved all of Michael's boys: silently and with self-loathing.

I watched them together and wondered why I was always watching him, him. Them.

So I sat on the sidelines, as usual, and refused to take part in their snugglebunny games. They smoked crack and jerked off for hours on end, while Jenny, Mavis, and I had tedious conversations in the next room. Waiting, always waiting.

Michael would emerge periodically, huffing and puffing and red in the face and blue in the penis.

"He's the one, James." And later . . .

"He really understands me."

It was a projection, of course. Michael needed to believe that someone could understand him, that there was someone else like him somewhere in the world, when it was obvious to me and all that he existed alone on a completely different plane than the rest of us.

Daniel wasn't "the one." He drifted out of our lives in due course, and was replaced by the next "one"—Bryan or Jeremy or Peter—I can't remember.

But they were beautiful, they were all beautiful.

Big ears and harelips . . . skinny puppy boys with soft eyes and . . . authentic acne!

Little boys.

He ate them alive.

I dreamed of those little faces that would fit in the palms of our hands . . . quick breaths, in and out . . .

A kiss, awkward and unsure.

Blushing

Dizzy

Flushed with emotion

Trace each rib. Count each hair.

Afterward, watching them—their energy! Their earnestness! The way they attacked everything . . . They were boys, real boys.

I remember one boy, in particular. This is true:

Twelve years old—a runaway . . . and who could turn away from a face like that?

Skin so smooth. And beet-red cheeks.

Why, he didn't look real. A little porcelain doll.

So Michael dressed him in drag.

"He looks just like Brooke Shields in *Pretty Baby.*" And he did.

A sexy little baby.

And the boy just loved it.

They would go to drag hustler bars and pick up old men for money. It was consensual I tell you—the boy loved it and got off on it.

"Go make Daddy some money." And off he went.

But it was funny and sweet and all so innocent. The boy had his moment and when it was over, he went back home.

And what is wrong with that?

And they came to him, they really did.

Nice job, if you can get it, right?

Still I loved them all. Silently, but with the knowledge that they weren't forever boys, that they would be gone and replaced again and again and I would never have a part of them. Once Michael had marked them, they were ruined for life. I could never have them and I would never know that feeling of being "the one," and being understood.

That was for Michael to feel and for me to watch.

But back to the general misery and humiliation that I was enduring with Mavis and Freeze ... They had to move—the robbery, the landlord, no radiator ... so they found their own little corner of hell—an ugly apartment on Eleventh Street. I hated it from the moment I saw it.

Its *feng shui* was all off: the ceilings were too high, and, *yes I'm aware that is usually an enviable condition in New York City apartments.* Here though, it just looked wrong. The room itself was long and narrow and it gave you the unsettling effect of living in somebody's hallway.

There were three bedrooms—each one smaller than the last—three doors lined up on the southern wall. One was a very large, spacious *boudoir* with a sunlit living area and a loft space for sleeping, one was your standard-size windowless New York bedroom, and the last was a hobbit's broom closet.

Mavis took the football field, OF COURSE (power-mad dyke that she revealed herself to be), and Freeze was relegated to the Japanese prison hot box.

The middle room was for rent.

Was this power positioning?

Did this arrangement cause any tension?

You bet it did. There were internal power struggles daily: they were both just too out of their minds to communicate them.

Freeze was a cracked-out basehead by this time; he didn't really mind *the room itself* ... the smaller, the darker, the filthier—well, the happier he was. He could sit in the dark and paint Day-Glo happy faces on the walls to his heart's content.

And Mavis was now a full-fledged speed freak, so nothing made her happier than pogo-dancing, UP AND DOWN, UP AND DOWN, for days at a time. She also found fulfillment in the construction of elaborate obstacle courses for her to run around.

Argh.

They were nasty sons-of-bitches, the whole lot of them. And there was a whole lot of them—people I didn't know or care to know.

For some reason it began to bother them that they were giving me hundreds of dollars worth of free drugs every night. They acted as if I were doing *something new,* and it upset them. About the fourth or fifth time of the night when I asked for yet another gram, their lips would purse, their eyes would narrow into little slits, and it would take them **A LONG TIME TO GET AROUND TO HANDING IT OVER.**

I would have to jump up and down like a monkey, and poke them and prod them and remind them how fabulous I looked that night, and just generally JUMP THROUGH HOOPS.

It wasn't fair at all. It was just damn rude, if you ask me.

Then, one morning, in the middle of a fabulous after-hours *soirée,* I asked for a teeny tiny little bottle.

And Freeze said:

"No."

Hm? What? *I didn't quite catch that.* And neither did you. WHAT WAS IT HE SAID AGAIN?

"No."

The room stopped.

And that *"snap, splat, gurgle"* sound you just heard? Well, *"snap"* was my heart breaking, *"splat"* must have been my ego being squashed, and that *"gurgle"* sound could only be the life-force draining from my body—Yes: *"snap, splat, gurgle,"* all at once.

That was when the Black Hole of Calcutta opened up and swallowed me. Good thing, too, because I would *hate* to have had to sit there, politely, and act like I wasn't humiliated. It would have been awful to have to make up some silly excuse as to why I was rushing out of the room, sobbing hysterically, throwing on a pair of tennis shoes, and going home.

Yea, I would have hated to go through that, boy.

How cruel. How rude. I mean, *really*, if you already owe five grand, what's another twenty dollars among friends. But they absolutely humiliated me in front of some *very celebrated junkies*, and I was furious.

Oh, now is probably a good time to tell you about a little problem I have with shoes.

I know this will seem like a long and pointless digression. (OK, I know it seems like *yet another long and pointless digression*.)

But when I was just a wee lad, a suckling babe in my sweet mother's arms **(yes, we're going back that far)** I was pigeon-toed. Exceptionally so. Comically so. I was forced into wearing special shoes that had an iron bar that connected my feet together.

I'm told I hated them. That's understandable, right? What child wouldn't?

I would bang them against the bars of my crib, all night long, and scare the bejezus out of my mother, who thought we were being burgled.

I'm going somewhere with this. I promise.

To this day, I don't like shoes. I hate shopping for them. I hate wearing them. It's a throwback to those torturous days and nights when I was shackled like the baby Hannibal Lecter.

I'm happiest barefoot. In fact, I pay so little attention to footwear that I willfully lose more shoes than anyone I know.

And very often, I get confused and forget what shoes are mine and what shoes belong to, say, *the person whose home I'm visiting.*

But that's just me.

It's a psychological block that stems from a childhood trauma.

I DO NOT INTEND TO STEAL PEOPLE'S SHOES. It just happens.

Let me reiterate:

Sometimes I get confused when it comes to footwear. I panic and grab the first pair of somethings that I see, and I PUT THEM ON MY FEET. Then I leave without giving it a second thought. THAT'S NOT STEALING.

It's delusional, catch-as-catch-can dressing.

Most everybody knows about this odd little peccadillo of mine. They know I don't do it out of spite. And they still love me.

I'm in a fugue; I can't help it.

A somnambulist's fog.

I become Bizarro James; the mad shoe-stealing James.

But later, you can always come to me and talk it over with me and I'll express my surprise, my shame, and my overall willingness to return the lifted item and do what I can to make up for any discomfort I've caused.

I'm that kind of guy.

All of this is leading to that fateful morning at Mavis's, when I put on the wrong pair of tennis shoes.

A simple mistake.

Except I had been wearing patent leather thigh-high boots with seven-inch spikes, *but, hey,* after three days and twelve grams of Special K, who can tell the difference? In my panic, they really seemed like something I would have worn.

So I took them.

Was it really that wrong?

Was it worth ending a beautiful friendship over?

When I got home, I took two Rohypnols and was out for the count.

I didn't hear the knocking at my door, or the screaming outside my window. I didn't know about the rowdy crowd of angry friends who were trying to help the poor, shoeless Peter-Peter Boyfriend Stealer back at Mavis and Freeze's.

But I **did** hear my window smash, and I felt a patent leather boot hit me on the head. I still have the bloodstains on my pillowcase and a disfiguring scar right there, on my temple . . .

MAVIS BROKE MY WINDOW, IN 30-DEGREE TEMPERATURE, WHEN I HAD NO HEAT IN MY APARTMENT, AND THREW A BOOT AT MY HEAD.

I heard peals of laughter and the sound of many feet running away.

It was the last straw.

It was so mean-spirited of her. So nasty and ill warranted.

It was officially the end of our sisterhood.

I mean, who knew Mavis had such a mean streak?

Who knew Freeze could get so petty and rude?

Well, I guess I did. I shouldn't have been naïve. They fought all the time and their fights had always been fearsome, frightening, unexpected. They came out of the blue, and always, but always, occurred at *the most unbelievably inappropriate times* — baptisms, bar mitzvahs, sweet sixteens . . . wherever we happened to be that evening pushing their wares. They didn't care. They were demons. Possessed.

I should have known they'd turn their anger on me someday.

But this! Breaking my window? Well!

It's just like them.

One time, I will never forget it, this was when we first met, they were fighting over a minor clerical error in their bookkeeping. Freeze didn't give a hoot. He was exhausted and all for just letting his generous nature and faulty mathematics slide for the night. "Don't worry," he said, "you'll get it back. I'll just eat the difference out of tomorrow night." Or the next night. No big deal. There was always more money out there to be made. He just wouldn't get those new chaps he had his eye on.

But Mavis wouldn't let it go. Oh no. She kept at him. Pecking away, trying to find out where that bag of coke went, and who owes what for how many grams of K.

Yada yada ya . . .

Skrinkle skroddle doo . . .

She could really get on a guy's nerves. Especially when the heroin and the roofies were kicking in and he was feeling so lovely.

But then, just as his eyeballs began their blissful roll into the back of his head and his oh-so-heavy lids began fluttering to a close, just as the warmth of that evening's leftover drugs began creeping through his limbs like a warm ray of sunshine—

Mavis pounced.

She beat him with her bony fists. "I want my fucking money, you lying, junkie, son-of-a-bitch!" She clawed at him, and pawed at him, and generally made quite a show of it.

Oh, lady! My!

This went on for about five minutes. He didn't even wake up.

Then she froze in midmaul, and changed tactics. I could see a lightbulb go on over her head.

She climbed off of him with an icy, cool resolve.

She picked up the plate of glass from the glass-top table and held it high over her head *(where she got the strength and the balance to do it, I'll never know)* but she just stood there, for about ten or fifteen minutes *(or so it seemed at the time)*, with the glass gleaming wickedly in her eye and that terrifying expression on her ugly old mug of *pure lesbian rage unbound.*

Then she brought it down—

SLAM!

SMASH!

—into a thousand little shards, that we would never fully pick up or account for... our feet were, and would remain, bloody nubs again for months to come.

Wow. What a sight.

Now, let me back up for a minute and explain that Mavis—poor provincial, aesthetically challenged little Mavis— *really only cared for three things in her whole entire life:* her waterbed, her five-piece sofa sectional, and her piss-elegant glass-top table with the granite gargoyle legs.

Oh, how she loved showing off her beloved home furnishings—the fruits of her labor! Each one, lovingly handpicked, then paid for with her hard-earned grocery money. These sacred items—her bed, her sofa, and her table—symbolized her independence, her taste, and her past. Three things she was tragically, and inordinately, proud of.

So you see, for Mavis to smash her beloved glass-top table like that—*well, you just can't imagine what it must have taken!* (Well, actually you probably *can* imagine: two grams of crystal meth over a four-day period, and one chronically irresponsible business partner, to be exact.)

But the raw emotion she had displayed! The sheer intensity! From whence had it come? In what dark corner of her soul had it been *hiding and festering* and waiting to show itself? How long had it sat, and counted the snubs and slights and personal affronts, before it chose to rise up and *explode in indignant fury:* *"NO MORE! FOR THE LOVE OF GOD, NO MORE!"*

Hmm.

Well.

As interesting a question as that is, there was really no time to sit back and chew on theoretical rhetoric. In a flash, after the shattering glass just narrowly missed hitting him, Freeze leapt to his feet. His eyes were blazing and his arms were raised in what every gorilla would instantly recognize as the attack position of the alpha male defending his domain.

Hello, who was this new Freeze?

What happened to the old one?

Why, not just a moment ago he was nothing but a bump on a log. A lobotomized sea cow. An utterly useless waste of leg room. He couldn't even fend off her puny little attack, much less retaliate with a counteroffensive of his own. I guess the K, the Rohypnol, and the heroin all decided to vacate his bloodstream at once, leaving Freeze suddenly stone cold sober and madder than a wet hen.

Look at *his* anger!

Look at *his* intensity!

Can it be measured? Can we gauge its depth and might? Can we chart it, plot it, figure it out, so that we can make sure that *it never gets too far out of control?*

The power of his emotions was staggering! Anything could have happened at that moment! *Why, he could have killed someone!*

In the months to come, I would see that look of rage again—many, many times again, once he became hooked on crack. But I never got used to it. And it always scared the beans out of me, *every time I saw it.*

So here now was my first glimpse of *yet another version of Freeze.*

I watched in mute horror as they slammed into each other with the force and fury of two Mack trucks colliding. My goodness, you might have thought the tectonic plates were shifting, or a herd of water buffalo was dashing through the East Village, such was the sound and the fury! Throw a kitten in a blender and you've got a pretty accurate description of what I was witnessing, ringside.

There was blood shed that day, and clumps of hair lost. An emotional hurdle was crossed, as well, and a precedent set.

A pattern was forming. It would happen again. And again.

After they moved into that awful, cursed Eleventh Street apartment.

—and Mavis began racing through her days like a rhesus monkey on a crack drip . . . shivering and shrieking and chattering away, for six or seven days. Hey, Mave! Thumbs up!

—and Freeze fell into his Freebase Free Fall (and was *so happy* for a time).

—when the bloom wore off the rose of their friendship . . .

—and the money got tighter . . .

They fought like this all the time. It became second nature to them. They fought until it was all they knew to do with one another. It was who they were now, what they had become: no longer Mavis and Freeze—*friends helping friends*—but two powerful, war-torn, politically divided, ideologically opposed mortal enemies, forever locked in the familiar box step of war. Loyalties were demanded. Sides had to be taken.

Their apartment crumbled beneath them. Or so I heard. I was still *persona non grata.* I imagine though, that dishes were broken. Furniture was destroyed. Nothing was ever repaired. No mess was ever cleaned up. A friendship was buried in the rubble.

I told you the place was cursed.

Then, suddenly, word spread through the clubs that they were on the verge of going out of business. It seemed the money was mysteriously all gone.

How could that be?

Well, you may recall that Mavis, too, fell pretty hard for the old Crack Rock and Pipe Combo. That, and, oh, the *seven or eight* OTHER cross-addictions that they had acquired together. I'm sure they don't even remember how much fun they had going broke.

It was gone now, though.

And since they weren't even *speaking* most days, they certainly weren't *coordinated* most nights. A fundamentally unsound way to run your basic Mom-&-Pop-type drug cartel, don't you think?

How was Freeze to know that Mavis overextended her credit with the supplier? And how was Mavis to know that Freeze left his whole kit and caboodle in a taxicab somewhere west of Brooklyn Heights? He lost all their money, all their drugs—in fact, he pretty much just *lost it period.* It was the beginning of the end for Freeze. Mavis, too. Neither one of them ever recovered from that deathblow.

Each one bottomed out separately and alone. Their friends had all been driven away long ago.

But where would they go? What would they do? If they weren't drug dealers anymore, how would they still be fabulous? Who would take care of them now?

Then Mavis got an idea. She saw a way out. She saw her savior, her little ray of hope.

She saw Michael Alig.

Mavis, *that crafty old coot*, convinced Michael she was the answer to all his prayers. She was the roommate he'd been searching for all his life.

God bless her.

I always knew she'd go far! I always knew she'd surprise us all in the end! . . . My gal, Mav! . . . I knew it from the moment I laid eyes on her! "That girl's going places!" I said. "That girl's got style!"

Of course, Michael didn't know of her financial woes, her crazy-ass crystal habit, or her propensity for mass destruction. He thought that maybe Mavis *was* the answer after all. Here was somebody who he hoped would look after him, cook up the rock for him, and maybe *even do a bit of spring cleaning* while she was at it.

Fat chance.

The Mavis that moved in with him was a bitter old drug addict who didn't give a flip WHO he was or HOW MANY times he was on *Geraldo*. Or so she said. That was *the old Mavis*, the country bumpkin who would slobber over any old Barney Rubble in a wig and twin set. By this point in the game she had fully figured out the basic rules of social interaction, and she was a **whole new Mav,** a whole new bag of chips. **Gone** was the perky little apple-polisher of yore, and in her place was a gravel-voiced, world-weary *femme du monde*. I tell ya, liver and lemons couldn't have tasted as bitter and as tart as our girl Mavis!

If you didn't know her, you'd swear when you saw her out

and about that she was a genuine, *Old School member* of the **highest, bitchiest order!** Yes siree. She had the part down pat. Why, if she had walked into the Limelight with Dianne Brill herself, I would not have been the least bit surprised. She was that good. To the manner born.

To Michael's credit, once he figured it out, and realized that it would be **HE** who would be taking care of **HER,** he accepted his fate stoically. In fact, they even made a rather touching couple.

COUPLE OF MONSTERS!

HA!

I didn't see her for at least a month after the devastating shoe incident. I only heard the daily rumors of her famous falling-out with Freeze, and her subsequent phoenixlike return to the top.

Then one day, I was walking down Thirtieth Street, past Michael's apartment, I don't know why. I was just pulled in that direction.

I didn't particularly want to see either of them, but I wanted *them* to see *me*—maybe looking out the window, or driving past in a cab. I wanted them to miss me.

But, damnit, there she was, surrounded by an all new entourage—strange, hippielike girls. I didn't recognize any of them. They were piling out of a van. I turned to run, hide, but it was too late.

"JAMES! DARLING! YOU LOOK FABULOUS! BIG KISS! BOTH CHEEKS! THAT HAIR! VERY JEAN SEBERG!"

Certainly not the reaction I expected, but hey, I rolled with it.

"Well, that outfit, Mavis, it's very . . ."

"You like? It was SO FUNNY. We were all going out with **Todd** last Saturday, and he INSISTED on opening up his boutique and DRESSING THE WHOLE GANG—*too adorable*—then when we got to Bowery Bar, Eric made us all give an impromptu fashion show! Well, afterwards it would have been *too heartbreaking* to give back all those memories, SO I BOUGHT EVERYONE THEIR OWN LITTLE TODD OLDHAM OUTFIT!"

Her little group squealed in appreciation and gave Mavis a BIG KISS, BOTH CHEEKS, as we walked inside.

Six months ago she was a sharecropper in Marietta, suddenly she's Betsy Bloomingdale?

"But, what? I'm trying to impress you? JAMES ST. JAMES? Enough about me, let's talk about YOU! Your favorite subject! Done anything interesting lately, dear? I haven't seen you out in AGES! But then, usually it's just Michael and me at Bowery Bar. Very dull, you know, but the food is free—Eric thinks we add ambience . . ."

They get comp'ed FOOD? At Bowery Bar?

Such a thing is possible?

She pulled me aside.

"Eight days," she whispered, "eight days on the *fiercest* crystal meth . . . !"

Click.

Of course.

I thought I heard a rattle! Why, she was just a big old Mexican jumping bean, clattering about. Her face was a death mask, skin stretched so tight it looked like it might snap off.

Crystal? *Blech!* And eight days? I don't have enough to do in my life that I need to be up for eight days. And there is *nobody* fascinating enough to spend that much time with . . .

I mean—you have to draw the line somewhere! At some point you just have to say: "Enough!"

But it looked as if we were friends again.

In fact, I followed her back to Michael's later that night and saw the sad reality of their life together. And it didn't look to be all Bowery Bar and impromptu fashion shows to me.

Quickly:

There's Michael and Mavis, living together in a pile of garbage . . .

Watch them move about, maneuvering from the bedroom, through the kitchen, to the living room. Hazardous going . . .

The kitchen has been ripped out. There is nothing but mortar, exposed wires, and piping. Sharp and rusty things lay about, inviting tetanus.

Somewhere a long time ago, in a moment of inspiration, when inspiration was still around, Michael had decided to COM-PLETELY REMODEL his condominium—the same condominium he hadn't paid mortgage on for three years. The same condominium that was in the process of being repossessed. But, ever the optimist, and always one for luxury, Michael ripped up the carpeting in the living room and buffed and sanded and lacquered the floors and—onward ho!—he completely rethought the kitchen.

French doors, of course, and new fixtures, new tiles; the sink should be over here, and the cabinets, well, the cabinets were altogether wrong.

Rip them right out. There and then.

And then—

Well, like I said, that was all a long time ago—when little things, like running water and refrigeration, mattered. The stove still worked, but then that was a perennial, a given, of course. How else would he cook up his cocaine? Those damn butane torches only lasted so long . . .

Look at Michael, will you? In his filthy old underwear—awful bouncing, bobbling things, falling all about—making us sick. He's all blue and wet and cold to the touch. Portrait of Michael as Clam Dip.

And Mavis, percolating nicely, *like popcorn on a skillet*—she is all over the place, pacing and racing about, barking orders to somebody about something . . . something . . .

Jenny, frozen, on a table, looking out the window. Waiting for *someone* to come. We don't know who, but *somebody* was bound to come along and cause problems. They always do.

So I was ordered to keep watch at the door. I was posted there to warn them of impending company—people who were probably on their way right now, as we speak, to disrupt their fun, break up their party.

I opened it up, to take a gander . . .

"Close the door! Close the door! What are you MAD, man? Through the keyhole! Look through the keyhole, for God's sake!"

So I was on my knees, forced to look through the keyhole, for imaginary friends and foes.

This is the first time I've ever seen Michael in such a state. It's hard to believe this is the same Michael who used to SCOLD me for indulging in a bit of cocaine now and again. Who would have thought he, of all people, would come to this? But, it makes for a rather gripping drama. Riveting stuff. It's hard to keep my eye on the keyhole. Impossible, when—

Suddenly Jenny did what Jenny was sometimes prone to do in those days: she ran out of the house, in a blind panic, into the cold autumn night without a jacket. She was just lost in the sauce, poor dear. Of course, it broke the monotony and everybody ran after her to give her the attention she was demanding. She might end up at the Russian Tea Room or she might end up in a crack den, who knew? Jenny's freak-outs were periodic, intense, and always *anybody's guess.*

These incidents were important, in that they showed her and us that the drugs were secondary, that we were a family first and foremost, and we would be there for each other, always.

She wasn't really craving butter beans that day in the trash can. She needed to know that we *cared* enough to drop the torch and find her a can opener . . . stop the madness and look for her shoes . . . thank her for her money and her support . . .

Give her a big kiss.

Another night, or maybe the same night.

Same situation, and same cast of characters: Michael, Mavis, Jenny, and me . . . others perhaps . . . Daniel? Peter-Peter Boyfriend Stealer? Who knows . . . Who can keep track . . .

Money—gone.

Drugs—gone.

Hope—dwindling.

Everybody! Empty your pockets! Give up that stash! Look again! Maybe you missed something the first three hundred times you checked. Still nothing? Who has a bank card? Checkbook?

How can it be? NOT ONE PERSON IN THIS ROOM HAS ANY MONEY LEFT? I find that hard to believe. Jenny, call your parents. Say you need . . . Books for school!

At three o'clock, Saturday morning?

Well, who can we call? Not Mr. Gatien. We'd already asked for "rent" three times this month.

Michael's credit at the crack house had been exhausted. *Michael's CREDIT at the CRACK HOUSE was exhausted.* And the club dealers were sick of us.

Uh. OK. Think.

Jewelry? Anybody have anything worth pawning?

Then.

An idea. The worst one of all.

The last idea at the bottom of the bottom barrel.

The antique grandfather clock. The one Peter gave as a Christmas present last year.

Who the hell needed that big old thing cluttering up the house? Who'd miss it? Wasn't there a clock radio in Mavis's room? That's good enough for Michael.

Somebody, somewhere would pay dearly for such a treasure. Why, you could probably get seventy-five or a hundred dollars!

So Michael, still blue, still wet, with the crack pipe still in one hand—with the help of Mavis—*dragged the clock* from door to door in his apartment building, waking up tenants, to see if they wanted to buy a grandfather clock—*as if it was all perfectly natural.* Neighbors helping neighbors. Of course.

Michael had a little story prepared, about needing money for a plane ticket or something—but his neighbors were apparently used to Michael, and his three o'clock *"emergencies."* At least this time he had bothered to put on a pair of pants.

Amazingly, *some tenants actually gave him money.* They always did. He could be very persistent, I suppose, or just riffling through the flour jar when their backs were turned and all . . . But he did pay them back. He put them on guest lists. He was famous. It was a funny story to tell your old college roommates when they called: *That wacky club kid you read about in the gossip columns, you won't believe what he did this time!*

I don't believe he ever sold the clock, but it's a helluva story, huh?

You see, you can look at this little vignette and take it for what it is: a typical problem all drug addicts encounter, with an atypical solution due to the goods and means at Michael's disposal.

Or you can look further and read into it a parable, an allegory maybe, a metaphor for how people and things were loved and discarded based upon their immediate value.

And maybe if we stretch it further, it could help us to understand how it was that Michael could agree to turn State's evidence on Peter later on down the road. How he could sell out his best friend and mentor.

But, quickly, quickly, let's not get ahead of ourselves.

We have Michael and Mavis, together, as *Grand Guignol.*

Here we have Thanksgiving at Tavern On The Green, both

of them under the lace tablecloth, taking quick hits off the crack stem. Here we have them being led out of the restaurant . . . shivering blurs, they were . . .

At hip little clubs, trendy restaurants, walking down the street . . . always, everywhere . . . lighting up their crack pipes, without regard to reputation or danger or possible legal retribution.

Until they were unrecognizable.

("This is what I've always dreamed of," Mavis had said nine months earlier, "Nothing could possibly go wrong . . .")

Michael began having crack seizures.

Just for the attention, I was convinced of *that*.

Always at the MOST INAPPROPRIATE TIMES.

During MY PARTIES, or whenever I started having fun.

The phone would ring—DRAT!—and we would have to move the party *once again* to the St. Vincent's waiting room. To jones and go through the motions of worrying about Michael, when we all knew perfectly well that Michael was indestructible.

Nothing could ever bring HIM down.

He would be released soon enough, and he would get right back on the roller coaster.

And certainly it was nothing major that signified his fall from grace. It was the little things, the ones I recognized from my own experience, that began adding up.

He stopped making nightly guest lists, an obsessive nine-year ritual that he dismissed without a passing thought.

He stopped returning messages, and when his answering machine broke, he just avoided answering the phone altogether.

It was a relief actually, when the phone company turned it off for good.

He had two cats, one of them a long-haired Persian named Spikers—a pug-ugly little thing, really—with a smushed-up face that looked like it had been repeatedly hit with a frying pan. But Michael loved it and spoke to it in Skrinkle Skroddles, and saw to its every need. That ugly-ass cat ate steak tartare while Michael and Keoki lived on Sweetarts. Spikers needed to be brushed and cared for daily and when I saw him with matted and dreaded fur, pulling at his skin and raising sores—FILTHY, HUNGRY, PA-THETIC—I knew Michael was sinking fast.

Keoki says he first noticed the irreversible signs of down-fall when he discovered Michael no longer took his teddy bear—Cozy Molly—to bed with him at night, and actually no longer even knew where the twenty-seven-year-old totem was.

In an article in the *Daily News* entitled "Fallen King of Clubs Still Aces With Mom," written after the murder, Elka Alig says she was the last to know about Michael's drug problem.

According to her she was SHOCKED to discover, in 1994, Michael's spiraling drug habits.

Her first clue was when Michael "didn't come to pick me up in a limousine" from the airport. She "knew something was wrong."

Then she found all those empty vials in his apartment.

"They're for my Lego," he reportedly told her.

Funny, I remember things differently.

Michael was always quite open with Mom about his drug use. In fact, I remember in 1994, she arrived during a massive binge and didn't bat an eyelash. We all carried on, business as usual.

"My baby looks so thin," she said.

"It's the damnedest thing, Elka," I replied, "he eats and eats, you know, but every night when they pump his stomach, he loses all those nutrients."

We all laughed.

"Are you at least taking your vitamins?"

"Well, Freeze cuts his cocaine with vitamin B12." he answered. "Does that count?"

And we all laughed again, and I wheedled another bag out of Mavis.

"Would anybody care for a line of vitamins?"

I can quite easily recall her asking Michael to send her some "nose candy" many times over the years. I even remember her doing ecstasy with her son at the Limelight.

But later, Michael told me that she said that I was a bad influence on him. ME. On HIM.

That's rich.

"My mother hates you. Every time she calls she asks if I still hang out with 'that old witch.' "

OLD?

I think it stems from that visit, when she fell into her first K-hole.

I suppose I was rather glib about it.

She was crying when they carried her over to me at the Limelight.

"Oh, no," Michael was saying, "I think she did Special K!"

She was disoriented. Couldn't stand. Couldn't talk. There was a look of terror on her face.

"Yep, that's a K-hole."

"What can we do?" Michael wailed.

I didn't offer my standard speech that I used to soothe K victims ("I know everything is confusing right now, but in only twenty minutes—yada yada ya).

Instead, I think I felt her up, looking for her stash.

"Just prop her up against the bar, Michael. Oh, by the way, do you have any drink tickets?"

Oddly enough, it was Jennytalia to the rescue. In a rare burst of taking charge, Jenny sidled up to Elka and came up with a stunning plan: "I'll meet you down in the hole and help bring you back. Michael, get her some cocaine to help break the high, and get me a half gram of K. I'm going down."

So Jenny is Elka's favorite, while I am the evil drug fiend.

Isn't life funny?

So.

If my incisors seem a bit exposed, and if you get hit by an excited spray of spittle as I rush to relay this next part of the story—watching Michael fall into the very same spiral of drug addiction that he used against me so often—understand that it was wicked of me to enjoy it like I did, but there was some ironic justice to be had.

Yes, this was the summer and fall of 1995, when crack was *le dernier cri*—and all the most fashionable folk downtown carried *butane torches* and *glass stems* in their Prada bags.

This was around the time of those posh penthouse parties that Peter would throw at all the chic hotels in town. Oh, you didn't know? You hadn't heard? Well, they were just BE-YOND, my dear. BEYOND ANY MEASURE ... Hedonistic pleasure pits! Drug-fueled orgies of epic grandeur! "Excess" doesn't even express! "Gluttony" is too kind!

Now, having said all that, I have to admit that I was never invited. Never. Not once. Oh, I suppose I would have been a buzzkill, a lone K-nut on a completely different wavelength altogether, stumbling about, looking to connect.

No, these parties were about freebasing. It's serious business, this— a group activity in which concentration, and dedication to the matter at hand, are paramount.

No time for trivialities during the preparation and eventual consumption of said rock. Conversation is limited to the quiet but insistent bickering over the proper rate of stem rotation and torch intensity. It could go on for DAYS. . . .

Clearly, I would have been out of place.

So all I know of those parties is what was told to me afterward: the naked games of charade, the tens of thousands of dollars worth of drugs spread out like a Roman banquet, the fort building with the fancy furniture, Peter, naked, patchless ... with one wild eye ... hiding behind the curtains—

Nope. I wasn't there.

The cheese stands alone.

But Mavis and Freeze and Jenny and later the new kids, like Gitsie and even Angel, I suppose, were all invited. And made the scene. And developed a taste ...

Crack was introduced to the club kids that summer, with such panache, such dazzling style, it seemed inconceivable that after a marvelous and worry-free binge, it might someday turn into, oh, *Jenny in a garbage can, hacking at a can of butter beans.* Who could ever imagine that it would change your personality, take away all that was good and decent in your life, including your morals, your friends, your furniture, your job . . . I saw it happen to everyone around me, but to no one more so than a certain spiky-haired lesbian tofu vendor from Massachusetts.

It became too much for her to handle. It became too much for *anyone* to handle.

Mavis left town. January '95.

She got out, God bless her, and tried to save herself by running blindly cross-country, looking to retrieve the soul that had been sucked out of her a year earlier.

I really miss that girl.

Meanwhile: Freeze.

He lost the apartment on Eleventh Street. He couldn't keep a roommate long enough to collect rent. It was dank and dirty and oh, full of *fish heads* and *crack smoke.* It was loathsome to visit, and detestable to live in, I'm sure. The crowd of baseheads who filled the apartment night and day were of such repulsive stock that it turned an already uncomfortable apartment into a true house of horrors . . .

Freeze was sinking into the quicksand: having lost his apartment, his status as a dealer, and the legion of toadying yesmen that came with it, he lost the will to dress up, go out, and have fun. In fact, he lost the will to make money, look for a place to live . . . even eating was beside the point.

When faced with eviction, he merely shrugged and slid quietly out the door without bothering to pack up his belongings. . . . Gone forever were the dozens of pairs of identical chaps, the armbands, the little leather vests, the platform boots, gone, without even a backward glance.

Thus we see the emergence of Freeze Number 3.

Remember—from his humble beginnings as the meek and mild milquetoast in Bella's back room, into his heyday as FrankenFreeze—we see now before us, Freeze Number 3, the fractured sum of that man.

Of course I took him in. I didn't have much of a choice. That's how it worked, for both Michael and me. Of course we had quite a racket going for a while there. Finding new drug dealers . . . tossing them back and forth to each other . . . We would shuck them, break them in, toss them back, and leave their empty shells on the barroom floor. But, of course, in the end we had to take responsibility for the destruction we caused. Of course we had to take custody of our dealers after we broke them. We both shared in the responsibility of housing and feeding them. Michael took care of Mavis long after she stopped taking care of him. I took in Freeze.

We would do the same for anyone, of course.

For better or worse, we were all family by this stage of the game, and like all families we were capable of monstrous acts of cruelty to each other. But ultimately, when all was said and done, we were each of us, all we had. In our own way we looked out for each other. You have to believe this, or I won't allow you to read any further. After all we had been through together, we all truly loved each other. And the worse times got, the tighter the circle became.

All of which is a roundabout way of saying that Freeze drifted into my apartment, my happy new swinging singles pad, and before I realized what was happening, he had dug in his heels, chased off my other roommate, and turned it into a reasonable replica of his Eleventh Street shithole.

In no time at all, my new home was a mess.

A mess!

And this—coming from me!

Me!

Who, very often, can be found just sitting in a dumpster, perfectly happy.

Me!

Well, I was fine with it even when it took the better part of an hour to navigate through rough terrain and stinking debris, to get to my bedroom. But when we had to call in the city plow to pave the kitchen with rock salt, I must say that I gave him a mighty mean frown.

Baseheads are a filthy lot.

He stayed four months, during which time we weaned him off crack and tried to rid him of his long-standing heroin habit. Three weeks in Dallas with our friend Brooke, *and he was clean as a whistle.* But once he got back to the city, he jumped right back on the horse.

Of course, of course.

When I'd had my fill of Freeze, he left and began his wandering. He quickly adjusted to his new status. He moved quietly, like a stealth bomb, you hardly noticed him when he slipped into your entourage. Before you could blink, he had thoroughly insinuated himself into your life—running errands for you, making you zippy little outfits.

Cooking and cleaning and organizing.

Just as sweet as pie. Wish he had been like that for me. I might have let him stay.

He would sleep on a pile of rags if that's all you had, and thank you gladly for the opportunity.

He didn't eat much.

He was rarely sad, and if he was worried about his future, and where he would go next, he never showed it.

And when it was time to leave, he would smile sweetly, thank you politely, and walk out the door (but always, always, leaving a bag behind, on accident, so when he was desperate, trapped, alone, on the street—he could call and retrieve it—then once inside your door, he stayed until it was time again to leave).

Many people avoided him when they saw him coming.

Many of the same people who used to kiss his bronzed and plucked little butt.

He saw both sides of everybody's worst side. From blatant ass kissing to the big chill in less than two moves.

Trust me, I know all about this: Once you've seen the absolute worst in everybody you've ever met, you sort of give up hope. Any good that you might see—well, you know better. You know what lurks beneath the surface, what's right around the corner. You've seen the truth in everybody. Everybody.

So you accept that everyone is inherently capable of hurting you. They're only out for themselves. You will end up hurt.

You can't judge people in the same way that you once did—"this person is good"; "this person is bad" . . .

You embrace everyone, equally—

But now there is a protective barrier.

So that's why Freeze would spend time with anyone. ANYONE. It didn't matter if it was the Queen of Romania or the Prince of Port Authority.

He was himself, once removed. When he was presented with something good, he took it quickly—because he knew it wouldn't last—and he steeled himself against the coming bad.

It's not such a terrible way to live. It's neither Heaven nor Hell. Because if you're never really sad—you know too much to let life surprise you or to get to you—then, you're also never really happy. That was the Purgatory Freeze faced as a street person, depending on his former fans to take care of him.

But I don't think he was bitter about his fall. Impassive, maybe. Philosophical, probably. Bitter, no.

In fact: there was a strength and dignity to Freeze Number 3 that was admirable, truly. He faced the unknown each day— rejection, hunger, withdrawal—without flinching.

He was broken, to be sure, but his blatant refusal to pick himself up, dust himself off, and get on with it, to find a home, find a job, get a life—well, it was breathtaking in it's audacity. He was, without a doubt, the most *imperious* vagrant you would see.

He expected to survive and, in fact, he did.

It was inevitable that he would end up with Michael. Mavis was gone from both of their lives, and with Michael's spiraling heroin addiction, they were perfect together.

After spending the summer and fall of '95 drifting from pillar to post, he landed at Michael's condominium just in time for Michael's eviction.

I mean, well, who *forgets* to pay their mortgage for three years?

And who else could get away with it for so long?

Peter was still willing to help. He offered to pay the back fees—but it was finally decided that it would be easier to just get another place. It would be cheaper in the long run.

So Michael and Freeze began house hunting together.

They clicked—*tic toc.*

And if you thought Michael and Mavis made a combustible pair, Michael and Freeze were nothing short of Hiroshima, *mes amours.*

Together, they brought out an oily quality in each other that usually was kept hidden.

Seeing them together, watching them work, made me shiver. They were like evil twins who spoke their own language.

And their syrupy sweet baby talk to one another, well it *was just plain spooky.*

Freeze, with a glue stick in one hand, a scrap of fur in the other: "Michael, Snooky, la-da-doo?"

Michael: "Yes, Freezeskers, lover-la-da?"

THAT, my friends, is the true heart of darkness. Speaking together in tongues—one mind, one goal.

I am reminded of a great quote by Stanislaw Lec: "I give you bitter pills, in a sugar coating. The pills are harmless—the poison's in the sugar."

Therein lies the basis of Michael and Freeze.

They had a systematic way of getting what they wanted, a sort of telepathy that instantaneously sized up potential victims, discreetly pointing out weak spots, Achilles' heels, any jugular veins the other swindlers might have overlooked.

They worked successfully together. (If you define "successful" as: *creepy, craven grifters*, then, by golly, they were at the top of their class.)

But the free fall was gathering speed.

They found a loft they both liked, and Peter paid the deposit, and somehow they forgot and left both of Michael's cats there alone in the empty loft *for weeks* before they moved in. When they decided against the loft after all, they remembered Miss Kitty and Spikers . . .

And ran back to fetch them.

Spikers was dead. Starved and frozen. Kitty was on death's doorstep as well, but somehow pulled through. Only to run away two months later. And nobody missed her.

THAT MICHAEL FORGOT AT ALL, and left his beloved Spikers to starve to death, shows just HOW FAR GONE HE WAS AT THIS POINT.

He and Freeze together were trouble. They doubled the dosage, increased their powers, and yet subtracted the whole of their former selves.

Michael and Freeze eventually moved back into the old River-bank apartment building on the West Side, where, years ago, Michael and Keoki and I had all lived as young and wacky neighbors. But those days were long gone. Michael was no longer . . . well . . . *young* anymore. There were still spurts of wackiness, but basically, it was sad watching that magical life force drain out of him because of the drugs.

Michael and Freeze hoped it might be a new beginning for them. A rebirth. They got a cute two-bedroom apartment, *well, cute until Michael got a hold of it.* Michael's taste was *very Ethan Allen,* if you know what I mean.

So.

It's September and the stage is almost set for the much anticipated *denouement* of our little Greek tragedy. Things are happening quickly now. Dark forces are gathering. Fate is about to intercede and change everything forever. It's coming. Soon. Soon. There still remains one element that is missing, but we'll get to HIM soon enough. I promise.

For now, let us merely gaze at the great tableau frozen in front of us, as the curtain slowly falls on Act II. The dust has yet to settle from the Mavis Mess, and the lighting here is so faint and gloomy, it's hard to make out what's going on. Some of the characters' actions are unclear.

We can *certainly* see the DEA circling about, trying to "blend in," to great comic effect. Big ugly apes in pearls and lipstick, awkwardly carrying lunchboxes. Apparently, the powers that be want Peter Gatien's head on a platter. And they'll sacrifice anyone's dignity to get it. There is a general sense of unease, almost paranoia, in the clubs these days. Many of the flashier people are crowded right off the stage. Others are relegated to the background. And then there's Michael, shrouded in shadows, blowing smoke rings from his crack stem.

Michael is on his way out, can't you feel it? Listen to the thunder of a thousand new hooves, a whole new generation of kids pushing and surging into the Limelight who don't know, don't care, don't want to know or care about club kid looks and clubland etiquette. Sorry, Grandpa—they just want to dance. They just want **KEOKI,** the **Superstar DJ,** who has pushed his way out of Michael's shadow, become a helluva DJ, and climbed into a lofty new position of power. It's his turn to take his rightful place in our Pantheon of the Painfully Hip. Keoki has dyed his hair *leopard,* RAR! and has a dozen "assistants" help him pick out which pair of chaps to wear to that night's gig.

But poor Michael is losing his touch, can't you see it? He's lost the will to go out and work the crowd, press some flesh, lure in those unsuspecting young pups into his lair. He has also lost his precious club kid magazine, *Project X* (it fell through the cracks, so to speak), and without that wacky bit of propaganda to fuel his fans' ardor, he loses not only his puppet-master's pulpit, but also a certain degree of validation.

The scene splinters.

Nothing seems fun anymore.

And amidst this chaotic disorder, amidst the clamor and clanging and changing of the guard, as the old once again despair to make way for the new—there, in the wings, waiting to make his appearance *is the last element of our story.* Yes! Over there! In the corner! Wandering onto our stage, coming into view, is one lone figure, one small figure, one terribly silly little drug dealer, all decked out in a pair of *wings!* Wings, of all things!

Here, now, pushing his way forward, up through the ranks, is a *third-rate Mavis* (if you know what I mean), demanding to be heard. This poor player wants his God-given privilege, as a **Club Kid Superstar Drug Dealer,** his right to strut and fret his hour upon the stage—then be heard no more.

Look, in the spotlight now, front and center: **the most important, yet least interesting character of all**—our aspiring corpse has wandered onto center stage!

LADIES AND GENTLEMEN, without further ado, as the lights go down, allow me to quickly introduce to you, THE ONE, THE ONLY . . .

Angel Melendez.

Oh!

I see *that* got Michael's and Freeze's attention! They seem to be looking toward the spotlight with undisguised greed. Notice them as they creep forward and circle their intended prey, all the while eyeing his large bag of pharmaceuticals, and the many pockets bulging with too much cash.

Tic-toc, see them smile and warmly greet and embrace Angel, as they lead him off the stage. And into the Riverbank. "Of course you can stay with us!"

Watch Michael and Freeze work to gain Angel's trust.

And that is how our story begins.

But before the curtain falls, let me leave you with one question—ponder it as the events unfold, then riddle me this:

If one day, Mother Teresa was out weed whacking and accidentally chopped off Hitler's head—**WOULD THAT NECESSARILY BE SUCH A BAD THING?**

I mean . . . if a person commits a crime, and no one cares—*can we all just adjust our lip liner?*

Look, I'm just being honest here. I think that the whole point of my story is that **nobody ever implicated *Dorothy* in the double witch homicides of Oz** because, well . . . you know. . . . *She's Judy Garland, for God's sakes,* and Louis B. Mayer forced her into a life of drugs at such a young age, poor thing . . .

Just remember that as we . . .

FAST-FORWARD TO...

THE AFTERMATH

I was an absolute puddle when I left Michael's house, just a big old body of water. How was I supposed to deal with this? *I'm no good in a crisis.* I fall apart when my mascara clumps. Defrosting my refrigerator is a traumatic ordeal. I freak out at ATMs. I spend hours agonizing over the phrase: "Objects in mirror are closer than they appear" . . . How was I supposed to deal with police interrogations, stalkarazzi, and the inevitable courtroom appearances—*because this will end up in the courtroom,* how could it not?

Oh, this was not an easy thing to digest.

I needed to do some serious thinking.

Very serious . . .

Serious, yes . . .

Now, where to begin . . .

Well, *Angel is dead.* Let's begin there. How do I feel about that?

I'm not upset about Angel, not by any stretch. He was a horrible person . . . my what pretty shoes . . . it's just that he didn't deserve . . . oh!

A string of lights sparkled on a balcony high and away.

Well, nobody deserves to die like that . . . and *why* did they have to use the Drano? . . . I don't think I understood that part . . .

Is that vanilla I smell? I really like vanilla . . . underrated, really . . .

Hmmm. Nothing seems to be sticking in my head. Blank slate. Empty cave. All the crowded, tangled thoughts that are usually diving and swooping around the inside of my head, like bats or too many pigeons, must have flown out my ear. I was alone in my head for once, and I did not like it.

Not at all.

I had made it all the way to Tompkins Square Park; I was thirty steps from my home. But I couldn't face making small talk with the blissed out ne'er-do-wells that were always jonesing on my floor.

I sat and watched pigeons peck at a pile of vomit, instead.

I hobbled around the park, through the wide open slopes of gorse and heather, pretending to be crippled—that always kills a few minutes.

I tried standing on my head, but as my head is completely misshapen—all isosceles angles, really—and the pavement was cold and sticky, and a crowd was gathering around me, screaming "You suck!"—I quickly gave up.

I know it sounds cliché:

But I'd start off thinking about Angel, and how an argument could get so out of hand . . .

I'd grapple with it for a good long while, really I would. And I would go in circles, until I finally just had to stop and wonder about something else, like *just why was it that Billy Joe MacAllister jumped off the Tallahatchie Bridge?*

Then I'd give the hammer issue another whirl, but would just end up wondering why FOX canceled a perfectly good show like *Herman's Head.*

And so on.

I dreamed I was Mary Hart—my hero—she of the marvelous million-dollar legs and soothing sotto voice. Oh, she is just my absolute *idol!*

Anyway, I was Mary and I was with my boyfriend, Dr. Dre— not the fat one. (Well, not the *really* fat one.)

Anyway.

We were kickin' it back in the 'hood, you know. The sun was shining and the Negroes were singing and *my hair was flipping so nicely* . . .

Suddenly we were all underwater—you know how dreams are—and I stopped being Mary and Mary became somebody else—*it all seemed so clear,* except that it wasn't clear of course, because we were underwater. Mary wasn't what she claimed to be, in fact she had a chainsaw and was busy hacking away at some sailor.

Well, it doesn't take friggin' Dr. Joyce Brothers to interpret *this* little vignette. Scholars won't be scratching their heads here. No need. It's just your standard post-Freudian pop imagery.

But this is odd: the upper half of the sailor floated by and I caught his thoughts. They were very calm. "Help me into the next place," he said, reaching. And, I too, felt a pang, a longing to go with him. Everything was warm and sad and joyous, too, and I woke up crying.

Reality can be a rather free-floating concept when there are three drug dealers staying in your apartment who owe you rent. Reality can be dismissed in the whiff of your nasal spray, the chopping of a razor blade, and the scoop of a straw.

And so it was in the days and nights immediately following Michael's disclosure. I went on an extended vacation, a much needed retreat from the world.

Three bottles of liquid ketamine a day... that's what I asked for, that's what I got...

...that cooks up to about four grams of K...

...this before I even went out at night.

I spent a lot of time on the ceiling. It's an easy place to be, once you adjust to it, once you acknowledge that you are, indeed, upside down, or maybe everyone else is, as well.

Of course, it doesn't really matter.

Sometimes there are three or four of everybody, sometimes they turn into my great-aunt Dessa; sometimes they just
float out of their seats and gently explode like little soap bub-
bles—

And as for those other matters, that distasteful bit
of . . . what?

It's gone.

This is my world now; insert fantasy here. A window opens,
it's beautiful. Go to it, ease into it, make yourself at home.
There's no need to ever come out. We still have two bottles to go.

And when that's gone, there's always more.

Life can be easy, when you hold the lease. If my friends the
drug dealers say no, it's their asses on the street. This is New
York. And I always have such cute apartments, people put up
with a multitude of my sins.

At night, at the clubs, I was a lumbering old lug nut. One
of those slobbering idiots I used to run from, myself, every night.
I had become a spastic mute so that I would be unable to give
voice to my building rage and frustration.

It wasn't attractive. It wasn't healthy. It was stupid. But,
then I never claimed to be Eleanor Roosevelt.

People, this is my sanity we're talking about. I was under a
lot of pressure.

The gossip had begun swirling in clubland. People noticed Angel's absence in that painful way they do when a drug
dealer isn't around to service them. Nobody cared about him
personally, but, shit, they needed that bump.

As the Gladys Kravitz of the New York City club scene, I
was expected to have an opinion on just about everything. I always reacted quickly and rather shrilly to the comings and go-

ings of the various club kids, to their surges in popularity, and their inevitable downfalls. You could find me on any given night, waving my arms in disgust at the whole lot of them.

It was no surprise then, that during this time people turned to me as Gossip Central.

"Did you hear? They found his head in the Bronx . . ."

". . . hands in a freezer in Staten Island . . ."

". . . face bashed in . . ."

"He was mugged in Harlem . . ."

". . . in the Witness Protection Program . . ."

"The *Post* said he was the possible victim of vampires in the East Village."

Everybody wanted my opinion; I always had my nose in everybody's business anyway, how could I not know something?

Rather than answer every question, rather than lie, or be evasive to every inquiring drag queen—it was easier to blast off on a rocket ride of K and fall into a trash heap someplace dark, where I could stay and pretend I was Cinderella sleeping in the ashes.

Everybody learned to leave me alone.

Eventually, it was easier to just stay home and feel sorry for myself.

I looked like hell. I was grumpy and consumptive.

Just imagine: skin like wax paper—thin and translucent—a web of purple veins throbbing and humming, just below the surface . . .

Nervous, clawing hands, grabbing at ghosts.

I didn't know where I was. I didn't know what was going on around me. Elizabeth Taylor could be River Dancing on my kitchen counter and I wouldn't have noticed.

So more, more. Cook up some more.

And I was drinking a lot. There were times when I blacked out and woke up screaming.

And always there was a crowd of people around to feed me more. The usual suspects: dealers, drag queens, hangers-on. Homeless club kids. No matter how much I needed to talk to someone about the evil in my life, it was never the right time, and just easier to do more.

And hope it all went away.

But of course it didn't.

Weeks passed until one night I was alone for the first time in forever.

Suddenly, there was a pain, here, in my stomach—a sharp *oomph* that didn't go away, it got worse, until I was on the floor, shaking.

I was hot and sweaty, but my skin was cold, ice cold. The pain was unbearable and I wanted to call an ambulance. The phone was off, of course. It had been disconnected for over a month. Anyway, after the last two overdoses, another ambulance and I could say goodbye to a lease renewal. My landlord was beginning to think we did drugs.

What was happening to me?

Food poisoning?

Was my stomach exploding?

Appendicitis?

I did what anyone would do, in such a situation: I crawled over to the Pyrex and scraped up some more K.

Shaking.

Dripping.

But: up and at 'em, into a grateful left nostril.

Then I waited, and as I slipped into K-land, I think the pain subsided. But who can tell, really?

Meanwhile, across the ocean *and halfway around the world,* somewhere in Germany ...

DIANNE BRILL—

The All-Time Supreme Goddess and Ruling Empress of Downtown—

DIANNE BRILL, who to this day if her name is whispered in some dark corner, three rooms away, Michael and I will SNAP TO ATTENTION, fluff our hair, spit-shine each other's face, and nervously shriek: "Where?! Where is she?!!"

DIANNE BRILL, who was probably appalled with club kid antics, thought they demeaned Downtown, and most likely held Michael personally responsible for the collapse of her empire so many years ago ...

DIANNE, who was living in Germany, for God's sakes, and hadn't stepped foot in a New York nightclub in ten years ...

According to Michael, Dianne heard about Michael's little problem—*I can't even begin to imagine how*—I think Michael made it all up to impress me—and on Michael's behalf, she called her ex-husband and Michael's former mentor, Rudolf. He supposedly sent Michael and Freeze some subversive sort of publication that discussed in depth how the laws work for the criminals, what to say during interrogations, how to get rid of evidence, etcetera. I think Michael was just making it up.

Nevertheless, Michael and Freeze hatched a plot. It was determined that Michael would leave the country, and, ACCORDING TO MICHAEL *(although I will never believe this was actually a serious course of action in anybody's mind but Michael's)*, he would go off to Germany and live out the rest of his years with Rudolf, making obscure European art films with Dianne. Can you imagine? *I was so jealous—that had always been MY DREAM TOO!*

But until the time came when he could feasibly leave the country, he would go to Denver and detox at Keoki's home there. That was the plan.

The following week, in the *Village Voice*, there was a sidebar to Musto's column which gave his plan an added urgency:

> *Here's the latest story going around about what supposedly happened in that recent club-land scandal: Mr. Mess was fighting with Mr. Dealer about money Mr. Dealer was owed. It escalated to the point where Mr. Dealer was choking Mr. Mess, just at the moment when Mr. Mess #2 happened to walk in. Mr. Mess #2, a quick thinker, promptly hit Mr. Dealer over the head with a hammer. Not happy with that, he and Mr. Mess decided to finish Mr. Dealer off by shooting him up with Drano—a trick even the twisted twosome in Diabolique didn't come up with. After Mr. Dealer died, the other two set to work chopping the body into pieces and throwing them into the river. "But I didn't actually kill him," Mr. More-of-a-Mess-Than-Ever has allegedly remarked (but he's unavailable for comment).*

It was the first official mention of the incident in the media, *and*, I might say, a pretty accurate report of what happened—*except that at this point*, sure, there was a lot of gossip—but no hard facts, and certainly nothing as specific as a hammer hit and some Drano.

After that initial piece in the *Voice*, everything just flew out of control. Life was insufferable. I was pelted with questions everywhere I went. Chased through clubs. Over and over again I was confronted with the question of "a club kid cover-up."

Once and for all now, let me say for the record that all this hoo-ha that's been made about the so-called circle of friends that *conspired to cover up the truth* and *protect Michael at all costs*, well it's just that: hoo-ha.

We didn't ask to be a part of his Blood Feast fantasy. We didn't want to be the ones to "make it all OK for him." We weren't in any positions to help *ourselves*, much less play nursemaid to the Black Hole of Downtown.

Michael has since said that by confiding in his friends, and involving us in every gruesome aspect of it all, it took the burden off him alone. "Now it was everybody's problem."

Well, *however selfish that is*, it just might have worked if he had a crackerjack team of razor-sharp specialists in his corner.

But Michael had us:

Gitsie
Jenny
And me.

There were others, later, but essentially he had us and we were all

deluded
polluted
diluted
And persecuted.

(Gitsie you may not know yet. She was Michael's latest girl of the minute—a sweet and sexy wild child. *Think Drew Barrymore for the movie.* . . . Saucy, sassy, hippy, happy—Gitsie was many things, but "capable" was not one of them.)

So there we were.

A bunch of emotional invalids, so disabled by our own demons that looking to us for help was like asking Christopher Reeve to "get off his lazy ass and help out with the dishes once in a while!"

I mean, what on earth could *we* do?

It took this Gitsie chick an hour to peel a banana, for God's sake!

And Jenny! LORD LOVE A DUCK—don't get me wrong—I LOVE HER TO DEATH. Sweet as pie. Pretty as the day is long. Gentle as a lamb . . . but how she makes it through each day without, you know, *falling in manholes* or *eating poisonous bugs* . . . I mean, just look at her! Her smudge-proof mascara is **impossibly** all over the place—on her teeth, on my walls. . . . *The girl is a mess.*

And me? I had vomit chunks in my underwear. I spent most of each day thinking I was Queen Victoria, traipsing around Buckingham Palace.

Not the ideal crew of spin doctors he envisioned, huh?

So if it was help Michael wanted, well, *whoops*, he was fresh out of luck.

If it was absolution he was after, we couldn't even *comprehend* it all yet, much less work out a moral position.

And if it was a drowning man's desperate attempt to drag us down with him—honey, we were already in the water and pretty much out of breath ourselves.

So this "subversive circle," and the underground railroad we supposedly provided, was really just a lonely group of losers who, for various reasons, did nothing but nothing.

We couldn't go to the police. Drug addicts don't go to the police. That was never even an option. They were the enemy—they harassed us, scared us, ruined our fun . . . gave us hives. No, no, no.

And besides, they wouldn't have believed us if we hobbled in, all rouged up, and bewigged, still reeling from last night's festivities. As a rule: club kids don't make credible witnesses.

Oh, we know the police had heard all the rumors. And they considered them to be just a bunch of third-hand allegations made by crazy drug addicts and drag queens, about a scumbag dealer and possible illegal alien—SO WHO REALLY CARED?

And note that in *every article* about Angel's disappearance and the growing suspicion of Michael and Freeze's alleged involvement—*every single one of the writers—from Michael Musto to Richard Johnson to Beth Landman to Frank Owen to A.J. Benza, and on down the line*—they ALL contacted the police and they all got the same response:

"WITHOUT A BODY THERE IS NO CRIME. THERE IS NO INVESTIGATION OF MICHAEL ALIG AT THIS TIME."

In article, after article, after article. No body. No crime.

So, short of donning my old frog suit and dredging the Hudson River myself, there were precious little options open to us.

And for some psychotic reason, Michael kept pushing back the date of his departure. I think he liked all the attention.

I *know* he liked the attention.

"JAAAAMES!" he screamed outside my window.

Oh, good Lord, no. Not now. Please not now.

"JAAAMES LA-DA-DOO!"

Whoomph. There it is again. That . . . unbearable pain . . . in my stomach . . . Quick, get me my K!

"LOVER! LADY! LA-DA-D'YOO!"

Please, no skrinkle-skroddles or logger blaggers at five o'clock in the morning.

"SKRINK HEAD LOVER, FLOP HEAD POODLE DEE POO!" He was singing and dancing in the street.

Oh, that's it. I just lost my lease. I can see my landlady's light going on. My neighbors are straining to look out their windows . . .

Can I hide? Can I turn off the lights? Will he notice? WILL HE JUST GO AWAY?

"HURRY UP! LET ME IN! THIS IS OUR LAST NIGHT TO-GETHER, FOREVER!"

My pain lifted. If only . . .

Sigh.

Just one more bump, then: "Will somebody stop his *cater-wauling*, and let him the fuck upstairs before I get evicted and my stomach explodes?"

He stomped up the stairs, leaving a trail of empty heroin bags in his wake. "Why don't you answer?" He sounded genuinely hurt.

"Give me a bump of D," I demanded. It was *the least* he could do.

"Oh, James—you know I need it more than you. Besides, I just ran out." He says this as he's doing two bags at once, a straw up each nostril—"Give me twenty dollars and I'll go get you a bag."

Bags cost ten dollars.

"Skrinkle. . . . Blag-lover. . . . We have to make *the most* of our time together," he tried a conciliatory cuddle, "I'm leaving tomorrow for Denver."

"*Tomorrow and Tomorrow and Tomorrow, creeps in this petty pace* . . . "

"What does that mean?"

"It means, you've been saying that for a month now, but you never seem to go anywhere, dear—except to the Eleventh Street corner to get your 'traveling supply.' "

He extended his lower lip and pouted loudly.

"I come here to *see you* and *spend time* with you. Oh, I give up. You are *SO* bitter."

"I am *SO* close to Eleventh Street."

"Sour as an old piece of rhubarb, that's what you are. Old and wrinkled and alone and bitter. But I love you anyway."

We hugged and I gave him twenty dollars.

PAIN. *OW.* STOMACH. STOP.

Two weeks later, he still hadn't left, and I was forced to attend yet another going-away dinner—his fourth—at Bowery Bar. Halfway through the appetizer, it happened again: the pain in my stomach came back. Rosemary's baby was feasting on my spleen.

I screamed and a mouthful of calamari flew out onto the table.

I slid off my chair and onto the ground where I proceeded to flop around in writhing agony.

"*Trying to steal my moment, James?*" Michael asked archly. "*Everybody, just ignore the Attention Shifter under the table!*"

"Help . . . me . . . !" I clutched at the tablecloth and sent wine glasses spilling.

"Really, James. Now you've gone too far. You're never going to see me again. Can't you let me just have ONE MOMENT in the spotlight?"

I wormed my way along the filthy restaurant floor, past the stares of disapproving patrons, to the men's room.

I crawled under the stall door and finished another vial of K.

That should get me through the dinner. I stumbled back to the table.

"Oh, I get it! Everybody look at James! *Poor James* couldn't get any attention, so he went off to do his secret stash of drugs! If you don't give me any—I'll tell the waiter to give YOU the bill. And don't think I won't."

"Gobble Dee Goo?" I responded, underwater.

"Oh, I could just kill you, James. Did everybody hear that? For my next trick I'm going to kill James St. James. Somebody call Michael Musto!"

But then, after months of faulty planning and aborted attempts, Michael and Gitsie finally slipped out of town that night, under cover of darkness and a cloak of silence.

A sneaky backdoor exit!

On the lam from Johnny Law!

Top Secret!

Never to be seen of or heard from again!

The plan was to rent a car and drive cross-country to Denver. There they would camp out with Keoki at Keoki's brother's house, and together they could all collectively kick their respective habits. Then, with clear and level heads, they would decide upon Michael's future.

But first, before he left . . .

Michael decided to meet with a reporter from *New York* magazine, and discuss his plans, his destination, and the reason for his departure. *Well, of course he did.* He volunteered all sorts of valuable information, about the selling of his new furniture, the highways and byways he planned to use to get to Denver, and, well, he basically left a blueprint the size of a billboard for the police and other reporters to come find him.

But what's the point of going on the run if nobody knows you've even left?

Michael's comments appeared the following week in a small item about Peter Gatien's continuing tale of woe. As if things weren't bad enough for the beleaguered club owner, what with the drug raids on his clubs and the impending state income tax audits, *now* he had to contend with the unwanted media attention his scandal-plagued, recently fired ex-promoter was bringing to him . . .

Even when he was out of the picture, Michael could still cause problems.

But for now, he was gone, out of my life, hopefully for a very long time. I could sigh, I might not cry . . . and I could try to get some sleep now.

The burden was lifted.

Out of sight, out of mind! ("Out of mind" being the operative term.)

My K-holes, you see, were becoming more and more fantastical, **more majestic, more *"de Millean"*** in nature. Whenever I went under, these days, it seemed I was forever starring in these *great biblical adventures,* where I played every role, I was in every piece of the set, I was the air we breathed, the film we watched . . .

It would be a shame to give up such a simple pleasure . . .

And it is because the heavens and earth had opened unto me, and because God had spoken and there were raptures and epiphanies, it was for *these reasons and these reasons alone,* **purely**

evangelical reasons, that I became a clinically diagnosed, fully dysfunctional, hopeless old drug addict.

I thought of myself as a slightly addled Sister Aimee Semple McPherson, preaching the gospel of K to the huddled masses. It was my duty to ingest massive quantities of K and to go into that shrouded, mystical world and bring back some nugget of knowledge to share with my growing congregation.

There were many groundbreaking, soul-shaking, heart-wrenching scenes that I wish I could share with you. I would wake from these dreams trembling—for I had seen the truth! The universe was naked before me, and I could see the naughty bits heretofore withheld from mere mortals. A very basic truth had been given to me, something urgent that I needed to understand.

Well, I don't have to tell you how sad I was whenever the cloud lifted. How I cursed lucidity! I lost everything, always. I needed to find a way to capture and record my visions. I wanted to share my wisdom.

It was in June that I began keeping my K diaries. Armed with a pad of paper and a pencil, I ventured fearlessly into the depths of the nether realm. I wrestled with elliptical concepts that had baffled mankind for years. I explored wormholes in the time-space continuum, tripped into the Horsehead Nebula, and rolled in globular clusters. I was a protoplanet in a meta-galaxy . . .

I awoke with palpitations.

What answers were revealed to me? What life-changing things had I written down?

Trembling, I opened the book and scanned the pages.

Did I dare even look? Could I handle the truth? Was

mankind meant to know the secrets I glimpsed in K-land? Yes! I owed it to humanity to read it!

There, on the page, scrawled, **scrawled!,** like a monkey writing with its toes, was what *three hours of labor* had produced:

If letters had eyebrows, these would be arched

Hello?! "If letters had eyebrows"? What was that? Where did that come from?

If pencils had necks, I'd wring them!

This was my *Sturm und Drang*? This was the foam and thunder that was the voice of God?

Maybe I just caught the ear of Providence at the wrong time. Maybe Divinity was in the bathroom when I rang. Maybe if I just duck back in the hole, I'll find Truth.

Of course, if K had wings, we wouldn't need straws.

It was a darker journey, the second time down.

I suppose it was all my mistake—the radio was on, and you **know** how I love my Lite FM. I've always said: "A day without Neil Diamond is like a day without daydreams."

It wasn't Neil, though, who serenaded me into this particular nightmare; it was the sad-sack sounds of Miss Juice Newton, who sang "Angel of the Morning."

For some strange reason, I don't know why, the words "Angel" and "Mourning" stuck to me as I sank into the cushions and began my reverie.

I was pulled down, instead of up, this time, and there I encountered Death and Misery, in all their blackened grandeur. Oh, those twin conspirators—always out to ruin my day!

It was all very red and wet and not the spiritual journey I was used to. Not at all! I don't remember the specifics, but when I woke up, I knew that I had dealt with something just awful.

I peered into my journal, and, written in chicken scratch, were the chilling words:

Evil must be baked at 650 degrees.

I was apoplectic, and I don't even know what that means . . . but I had goosebumps and tears in my eyes . . . What a spooky thing to write down!

I shook my head.

It all had something to do with long stretches of cracked earth and the spirits that escaped from them—and things being two things at once, which I knew, but didn't want to acknowledge.

Then . . . oh, is that Kim Carnes? I just love the timbre of her voice . . .

Where was I? About to do another bump, that's for damn sure.

First one nostril. Then the other. And now . . .

K-HELL

I am trapped in a hole that has no meaning, and I could very well be there forever.

I don't even know who I am, or how long I've been me, here. There.

It is pure existentialism. No beginning, no end. Just a now that forever yawns ahead.

It's an awful place—methodic, formulaic, routine, full of carefully thought-out corridors that intersect and bisect and run both parallel and perpendicular to each other.

I accept that I will never understand it, and I will never know where it is, and it will always be like this.

It won't ever stop.

It will go on forever. And I will have been here forever.

There are pipes, dripping pipes, stacked on top of one another, that lead down darkened hallways,
and separate,
and come together again.

These pipes scare me; they're dripping and they're cold and they go on forever.

I follow one and study the coils around it, and the valves, and the faucets and pressure releases.
. . . increasingly covered with sludge and algae . . .
and there are bricks—dull and chipped—

Now, I am being wheeled through corridors on a cold metal gurney—and there is only the pipe to lead the way, to hold on to, the only thing that's constant, as darkness settles and the corner turns become sharper as we make our way deeper into the labyrinth.

PARTY MONSTER

There is sound—a hiss, a drip—then metal scraping, loudly, and then there is *only* noise and nothing to see, although there must be hundreds of pipes converging, coming together, all of them tangled and hissing.

I can't scream. I can't see.

I'm strapped down and I panic, I struggle, but the more I struggle, the tighter I'm bound.

I don't understand.

I don't know where I am.

I don't know who I am.

And then.

Someone else.

A breath on my face—cold—and close, it must be very close. Almost on top of me.

And again I can't scream.

There isn't movement.

There isn't sound.

Just a steady breathing in and out, cold on my face.

And I know who it is, but my mind won't take it in, won't absorb it. And this moment lasts forever.

I am still there.

For even after the K-hole breaks and I come back to the surface and I am safe at home with all that's familiar, I know that he's still with me.

I was THERE
and I will return

and it will be just the same
and I will have never left.

He comes to me now at night, when I sleep. I don't need the K anymore—he knows how to find me without it.

And so he comes to me, in the dark, always, and I feel his breath, uninterrupted, on my cheek.

I can scream, and quite frequently do, but I can also lie still and accept that I have been chosen. A reason is forming.

The fear is a gift.

He has brought fear to me. It stays with me, even in the daylight, even when I think that I'm happy.

Night after night.

Until I begin to crack. He's in every shadow, in every corner, in every thought.

And then, suddenly, one night, the breath stops short, is interrupted, and then is gone. And it hits me. The magnitude, the enormity of this interrupted breath.

He's gone.

And his absence is much worse than his presence.

By now it is June and I cry quite openly, most days—but I don't dare explain.

And then there were times when I was bad, or the times were bad, and I was punished by God. There would be a drought of K, and I would panic, of course, and I couldn't cope.

Tiny beads of blood rained red on my face.

And my stigmata would start acting up.

If days went by without a bottle, or a bag, or a bit of a bump—the veil wouldn't lift, clarity didn't return, and there was no cold slap in the face. . . .

Reality was no longer the opposite of K.

Instead, things got murkier, muddier. I had bouts of paranoia.

Now—in the past—when I felt plucked and pulled and put upon, I could always escape, and hide in the bathroom. It was my Valhalla. My safety zone. My worry buff. I would crouch in the corner for hours, days, until the bad feelings went away and I was myself again.

Not anymore.

Lately, the eyes in the bathroom walls glared at me from their oak-knot slots. And the shapes there in the wooden patterns were not for my understanding anymore. *Even the toilet frightened me*—a face appeared, there, in the bowl . . . a watery, old biddy . . . who MADE IT VERY CLEAR that she didn't want my butt in her face.

I wasn't welcome there anymore. I had nowhere to hide.

Worse: the far-off murmurs I always heard, and usually

lulled me to an even keel, weren't voices at all, *but computer squelches* speaking in a bitchy binary code meant to exclude me! It made me all googly-eyed and wobble-dee-blagged. My head hurt and I couldn't think straight.

Needless to say: I needed my K. My lightly toasted animal tranquilizer. My own personalized Prozac, if you will. (I'd have tried the actual stuff, but Prozac is **SO,** like, '91.) Oh, I needed that K, badly, no doubt about it.

And nothing could be right until I got it. And God help the poor roommate or friend who didn't move heaven and earth on my behalf. I made Nancy Reagan seem positively CUDDLY in comparison.

"SOMEBODY FIND SOME GODDAMN K FOR ME! *I DON'T CARE IF YOU HAVE TO SUCK IT OUT OF A SICK CAT'S ASS AND PUT IT THROUGH A DISTILLERY!* Just . . . do it."

Michael had only been gone a couple of days when I started hearing certain discrepancies in his version of what happened.

The sun was shining rather rudely into the cab, and traffic on Avenue B was at a Pinteresque standstill.

There was a continual gag in the back of my throat, like I'd been swallowing a ball of string all night (we were on our way to Save the Robots, and goddamnit, getting there was *not* half the fun). Nobody had much to say, as visions of ice-cold screwdrivers danced in our heads. We waited and timed the traffic lights and stole secret glances at each other's greasy, blotchy, pimple-ridden faces. It was all very nerve-wracking, until Peter-Peter Boyfriend Stealer broke the silence with something *nobody* expected:

"Of course Michael and Freeze didn't do it . . . I mean, *of course* they didn't . . . but I was over at their house the day before the argument and Michael was all cracked out of his mind, and all he kept saying was, 'Let's kill Angel . . . Let's kill Angel . . . How can we kill Angel and take his money? . . .' Isn't that a weird coincidence? I mean . . . *of course they didn't do it* . . . but the VERY NEXT DAY ANGEL DISAPPEARED."

Oh . . . my . . . yes . . . that *is* an odd coincidence . . .

There was a total eclipse of the sun just then, I think, and the cab started rotating in breakneck concentric circles. Or maybe the earth fell off its axis. SOMETHING odd happened, that's for sure, and it was many hours before I could focus and find the wherewithal to perform my many how-do-you-dos and perfunctory curtsies to the denizens of Save the Robots.

Peter's passing remark had planted quite a bee in my bonnet, and its buzz drowned out any fun I might have had.

EVERY LITTLE BREEZE SEEMS TO WHISPER: "MICHAEL AND FREEZE."

Another day. Another cab. When we pulled up to the light, a blind leper in a wheelchair squeegeed the window. It wasn't a first-rate squeegee, as far as I was concerned—and it *certainly* didn't merit the whole dollar my driver surrendered. I'm very particular about these things, and I *so dislike* getting into discussions about the right and wrong way to clean a cab window. That's why I cringed when he wheeled over to me and tapped, ever so sincerely, on my window.

I rolled it down and half-heartedly began explaining that a *simple back and forth motion* always works much better than a *random round and round.*

"No. No. I don't want your advice or your money, man," he rasped, "I . . . want . . . you . . . to . . . **DO THE RIGHT THING.**"

The light changed and the cab peeled off.

Now what do you suppose that was all about?

I pondered it for a moment or two, then went back to wondering if perhaps the **reason** for my depression *was a lack of niacin in my diet.* That would certainly explain my crying fits. I couldn't even make it through those commercials for cotton anymore without. . . . Hey.

The cab had stopped.
Just stopped in the middle of the street.
The cabdriver was looking neither here nor there, at nothing in particular. He had just decided to drift off into dreamland.

"I do it all the time," he said presently. "It's hard enough out there, isn't it? I never know the right way to go. Sometimes, when it gets too rough—I just switch gears. I turn off everything and just sit." *Pause.* "But you can't do that forever, James. People suffer from indecisiveness. You have to do something. You have to do the right thing."

I thanked him profusely, then gave him his money and a healthy tip. How he knew my name baffled me—but I guess I just look like a James.

Were these two incidents mere coincidence?

A benevolent leper bent on reforming me, and a dreamy cabdriver who only wanted what was right?

I thought so. At first. I was at the Christopher Street pier, and so I sat at its edge and stared deep into the murky water of the Hudson River.

That's when a pair of lips floated by and gurgled what sounded like "Yo, James, help the Brother Man. He's down here and he needs your help."

Before I could scream, one eyeball surfaced and glared at me accusingly.

Yes, something was afoot. And it wasn't just that lone foot bobbing in the waves. Someone was trying to tell me something.

It's true.

Later, my alphabet soup spelled out: "WHAT? YOU'RE WAITING FOR SOME SORT OF DIVINE INTERVENTION? YOU SPINELESS WORM—GET OFF YOUR SORRY ASS AND DO SOMETHING!"

And when I sat in the park and looked at the clouds . . . they formed their usual little ducklings and piles of cocaine—

but then I saw an Asphyxiated Colombian drift by, and then an Apathetic Judicial System rolling past in a tumble of cumulus clouds.

What did all of this mean?

I went to the Gypsy fortune-teller on Avenue B and Fifth Street, and she looked long and hard at the palm of my hand, she peered into the darkest regions of my soul, she searched the many hallways of my heart, and finally uttered the words:

"NOBODY REALLY LIKES GIRL SCOUT COOKIES."

That . . . was . . . my . . . last . . . K-entry . . .
It was one of those *Celestine Prophecy* moments.

When it came—when it finally came—the moment of clarity, when my fragile little mind grasped the whole ugly truth, and *really saw it for what it was*, it was like being awakened with a punch in the nose.

I was stunned.

I leapt up from the floor: "Where am I? What happened?"

Then I noticed the blood on my hands (metaphorically speaking), and the pain that seeped through my every pore. I was wet and angry and scared all at once.

But it felt good. It felt real. And facing reality gave me a sense of purpose . . . and more energy than a week's worth of Mavis.

I had spent months slumbering in the poppy fields, AND NOW I WAS AWAKE AGAIN—battered and bruised, but AWAKE—and ready to do something.

First thing first:

I had to connect to people again. I had to talk about it. I had to dissect it and figure out where I stood and how I was going to deal with it.

No more hiding my head in the sand.

So, I spoke freely and held nothing back.

To my landlady: "Judy, I'm sorry the rent is so late, but my best friend chopped up his roommate and I chose denial through drugs as an escape from responsibility."

To the deli man: "Turkey on a roll, with provolone and just a little bit of mayonnaise—by the way, did I mention my friend Michael murdered Angel Melendez?"

To a random stranger on the street, walking his schnauzer: "My what a sweet doggie! *Yes! Yes, you are!* Aren't you just the sweetest little thing! I bet *you'd* never inject anyone with Drano, would you? No siree! Not a cute little doggie like yourself!"

Clumsy attempts by anyone's standards, to be sure. But, still, it was a beginning.

I tried telling someone with a closer connection—my roommate—a nervous fellow named Tim Twin.

"Whatever you do, DON'T TELL ANYONE."

But I don't think he took it very well.

When I left the apartment, he was a light blue color, and vibrating in an unhealthy way.

Jenny, of course, was no help at all. Her standard reaction to any situation—be it the dismemberment of a friend or that she was out of Blueberry Pop-Tarts—was a free-flowing series of nonwords.

When I tactfully suggested my suspicions to her, *that maybe there was more to Michael's story than he was letting on*, well, she chewed on her carrot stick long and hard. This was her well-thought-out response:

"Oh, I know, my God, I am, like, just freaking out." This, in a D. deadened drawl. "And, I've got this paper due . . ."

She was with her standard coterie of wastrel junkies and disillusioned youth, all of whom already knew the score. (Jenny gathered these gentle junkies in the park and clutched them to her bosom—*swell bunch of kids, don't get me wrong, but I'll be damned if any of them could conjugate either . . .*)

"Yea, it's. Like, so fucked up," they slurrily concurred.

"I was, like, 'Oh My God.' "

We all sat and looked mutely at each other, until Roger, the Heroin Dealer showed up. When he left, we each did a bag and that gave us the confidence to talk about it some more. We vigorously debated the issue between naps.

When the strand of drool from Jenny's mouth threatened to extinguish her cigarette, I knew we had taken this exciting conversation as far as it could go.

"Well, this is going nowhere," I said.

Ten unfocused eyeballs turned away in shame.

"What are we going to do? This is really upsetting me! Jenny? . . ."

"I know . . . ," she tried, "I've just got like so much home-work to do, you know?"

"Jenny," I pleaded. "Face the facts! We have to deal with this! Hiding your head in the sand won't cut the mustard anymore!"

Oh, what a singularly unattractive quality denial was. Jenny looked like a retarded duck. I hope I never live to see the day when I am that out of touch with reality . . .

I took one last look at the lot of them, shifty drug addicts all, and spit on them (actually, I just sort of drooled heavily in their general direction . . . BUT THE FEELING WAS THERE).

Walking with Freeze, down Avenue A, because when I saw him he was so down, so out, so sad, so lost—like a pawn in a game he didn't understand—and even though a simple "Hello" meant an automatic four-day stay . . . how could I turn away from him? Now?

We talked of meaningless things, of cabbages and kings. Our vapid ways and numbered days. I was too numbed by what I suspected to even question him at this time.

Though we didn't talk of Michael and his departure, there was a sense of finality on Avenue A—you could see it in the way people like us carried ourselves in the heat, shoulders stooped, deflated, no longer willing to pretend, or try, or fluff our collective hair and put on some metaphorical lip gloss.

When we saw Brooke, it broke—the mood—it broke, and we collapsed into each other, like there might be hope after all.
But no.
"Did you hear?" she said. "Someone named Frank Something or Other is doing an article about Angel—front page!—for

the *Voice!*—And apparently somebody has come forward with
some kind of proof about Michael, and you, and something
about . . . oh God . . . I don't remember but it sounded major . . .
Isn't that scary?"

Freeze merely shrugged.

Past the point of nail biting, I suppose.

Past the point of worrying when the other shoe would
fall . . . because falling shoes ruin everything, always. But Freeze
didn't care about falling shoes any more than he cared about the
price of tea in China. It was all over for Freeze anyway. This was
all a postscript.

But for me.

For me it was different.

I still cared and that changed everything.

If there was really some sort of irrefutable evidence of
Michael's wrongdoing floating around out there (A taped phone
conversation? Possibly. Somewhere in the DEA wiretapping
tapes?) . . . And if this person, whoever it is, was going to the
press with it . . .

Well, that certainly upped the ante, didn't it?

Now, legally, we were all implicated, weren't we?

And some sort of action had to be done, *to protect ourselves,* not Michael.

Scrolling through my head was a blinking red-letter list of
charges I might face: Accessory to Murder, Aiding and Abetting,
Collusion, Obstruction of Justice, Conspiracy, Failure to Report
an Accident . . .

Would I be questioned, taken in, charged? I would need a
lawyer and money. All this involved commitment and sacrifice. It
meant *coherency* for once, and extended bouts of lucidity. I would

be asked silly, useless, and forgotten things—like facts and details and dates.

It would be hell.

(But then, of course, there was a fleeting glimpse of a grand courtroom entrance ... me, in a large veiled picture hat over a tastefully tailored navy dress. Stark. Sincere. Maybe a strand of pearls and an embroidered hanky ... Breaking down on the stand as I tearfully confessed all. Then: Redemption. Public Approval. Diane Sawyer.)

But mostly it would be hell.

I looked at Freeze—I was with Freeze, you see, so I looked at him—and said:

"Knowledge is power. It's important for everybody on all sides to know exactly what's going on and where we all stand. Who knows what. Who is working for and against who. It would certainly benefit you to know what information is being passed around, and what this story is going to be about ..."

(And privately, I was thinking that knowledge gave me the power to preempt any press I might get, and remove myself from the resulting "guilt-by-association" stigma that inevitably came from being involved in a scandal. Selfish and ugly, I know, but my Old School instincts still occasionally rear their manipulative heads.)

So we went to a pay phone and called Frank Owen at the *Village Voice.* I had known him forever, and had helped him out on a number of nightclub-related articles in the past.

When I said I was with Freeze and we wanted to talk, he *whooped* and realized "scoop" and said, "Come over now."

By bringing Freeze in, I was first and foremost helping Freeze. I knew he wasn't going to say anything damaging, and this gave him a chance to set his story up and to find out just how bad things were getting and if maybe it was time for him to get out of town as well.

And I was helping Frank, of course, by handing him the elusive "other factor" in the case—Freeze. Up until now, no one really knew anything about the mysterious hammer-swinger. Now Frank was definitely one up on the competition. Here was his big chance.

So my attitude was:

"I give you Freeze. Interview him now and be thorough, because I guarantee he'll never talk to the press again." And I was right.

In exchange, we just wanted to know the latest developments, as they happened.

So we went to the *Voice* offices, into a locked room. Frank recorded the conversation. I started off with a quick rant about Angel and his inherent loathsomeness.

Then Frank asked Freeze a few questions.

Freeze was quiet and spoke in halting, short gulps. No, he didn't know where Angel was. There was a fight, an argument; Angel left and they never saw him again.

Frank let it go at that, then brought up age-old rumors, about the other dead bodies that Freeze always ended up with; long-forgotten friends who had overdosed here and there, nothing that didn't happen to all of us, all the time, and very much beside the point.

Frank didn't grill him very hard. And poor, put-upon

Freeze was the very picture of innocence that day. There were no dramatic revelations, no cagey games of cat and mouse. I realized, with a sinking heart, that Frank must have thought it was all just a hoax after all, a club kid publicity stunt, and consequently nothing would come from this.

So all of this was just a pointless exercise in the dispensing of noninformation to the media. We would all become masters in the months to come.

We left after an hour or so of small talk, and as we hailed a taxi, Freeze turned to me and said: "Can you believe all this? Can you believe what's happened? What we did?"

It was the first time he had addressed the subject to me, and acknowledged my knowledge of it.

"Pretty big stuff, yea," I said. Well, I mean, what *do* you say?

"It's all Michael's fault, you know. If he had just kept his mouth shut. *Oh, I could just kill him.*"

That hung in the air for a good minute or so, then we both laughed long and loud—our nerves were frayed.

He came home with me, which meant that I had now inherited him for a week or so.

There was a note on my door from Jenny, telling me to rush over—"URGENT!"

When I got there, she was clearly shaken.

You see:

She was working at Trash & Vaudeville, when she looked up *and saw Angel standing there.* And she just, "like, you know, *freaked out.*"

Of course it wasn't really Angel, it was Angel's brother, Johnny, a dead ringer. He was handing out fliers: "Has Anybody Seen This Person?" with a scowling picture of Angel, in patent leather and considerable wingspan, and mention of a four-thousand-dollar reward.

Johnny and Jenny talked for hours—well, mostly he cried and Jenny stuttered soothing non sequiturs.

He gave her his number and said he NEEDED TO TALK TO ME IMMEDIATELY.

Oy.

So I called him.

I had to.

I wished that God would have taken me right there and then. A bolt of lightning perhaps. Or some killer bees would have been nice. Nothing could be as painful as this one phone call.

But he was sweet—so, so sweet. And sad and confused. He loved his brother, *well of course he did,* and he missed him. He didn't understand all this club stuff, he didn't understand his brother's lifestyle or sexuality, but he loved him, like a brother should and

HE JUST WANTED TO KNOW

Was it true? Was he dead? Did this Michael Alig person or this Freeze know something? Were they involved? Could they help him?

If it *was* true, he didn't care about them . . .

He didn't want revenge . . .

"I'm a good person. I have a family. I don't have time to hate anybody. I don't want revenge."

Whoever did whatever to his brother he didn't care. God will take care of it in the end. It wasn't his place to extract justice.

"I just want to know. To put him to rest. To grieve. To tell my mother. And to find the body and give it a proper burial."

That was most important. A consecrated burial.

The family couldn't go on with their lives until they knew the truth. Until then *every day was unendurable.* Questions, doubts, hopes, fears. Hand wringing. Every time the phone rang, every time they turned on the news . . . *Was it true? Was he dead?*

Please.

Could I help give them some closure?

He started crying.

It was the first honest, heartfelt, outpouring of grief I had heard on Angel's behalf—and I was paralyzed.

As long as Angel stayed an abstract, and unlikeable, symbol—the murky, misplaced modifier in some far-off subordinate clause—I could digest his death in small bits.

But here was a family who was suffering. A mother had lost a child. A brother lost a brother. But they couldn't yet grieve.

"I . . . don't . . . know . . ." I said dully, without emotion, "I wasn't there. I don't know what happened."

But.

Here was a chance. To do something.

So: "Johnny, I can't help you. I'm sorry. I just can't. But there is someone who might be able to. His name is Frank Owen and he's doing a cover story on your brother in the next issue of the *Village Voice.* Maybe it would help both of you to talk to each other."

I hung up, after giving him Frank's phone number, and felt sad and unclean, but slightly better.

Perhaps Johnny's raw and desperate plea could change the tone of the article, make Frank see it wasn't just Michael's usual monkeyshines, and the story would spark an honest-to-God investigation.

(In fact, if Frank were truly convinced the rumors were all true, then maybe HE could tell Johnny that, yes, his brother was dead and that the body was irretrievably gone, and to try to grieve and find the closure they needed WITHOUT the burial.)

I called Frank and left a message asking to meet him again, alone, so we could talk.

Now Jenny and the Junkettes were listening to all of this, and they were slack-jawed.

There he goes, there goes James—manipulating the media, betraying Michael and all to further his own press-hungry agenda. I was Frank's Deep Throat.

At least that's what she told people later—that's what I heard she told people—although that's a lot of words and a lot of emotion to come out of Jenny at one time.

And this only added weight to the theory that *I was the one* who started it all with Musto's blind item. Not true.

It depressed me terribly.

And I truly felt for Johnny. Mind you, I wasn't about to get carried away with emotion, though. I was not going to help confirm sainthood on some stingy, drug-hoarding bastard. I'm sorry. Johnny was sweet, but all wrong about his brother.

LETS TALK ILL OF THE DEAD, SHALL WE?

Johnny claims that Angel carried a hundred thousand dollars around in a duffel bag—and that he planned to quit dealing drugs to pursue a career in the arts.

Right.

Angel had a hundred thousand dollars in a duffel bag. *He's homeless,* but he has a hundred thousand smackeroos that he leaves in care of Michael Alig. Even Angel, social-climbing Angel, wouldn't be that stupid. He has a hundred grand and everyone still hates him. That much money and he *still wouldn't give me a bump!*

Think about that, will you?

And the bit about how he was about to retire. How cine-matic: "Just one last job. Just one more heist . . . if I can just make it through the week . . . Then I can retire and take care of my indigent mudder in Colombia . . ."

And, of course, he doesn't make it.

Let's face it. Drugs are what gave Angel his clout. It had his idol, Michael Alig, jumping through hoops. It got his dick sucked. It let him get away with being the cocky son-of-a-bitch that he was.

He wasn't going to give that up.

He wasn't going to go away.

Yea, yea, yea—he was going to be an actor. Or a writer. Or a singer. Yea, yea. So was your grandmother. And just look at her.

I hate to be cynical, but Angel didn't have a hundred grand, he wasn't going away, and he was never going to get out of the vicious cycle of dealing. It was all he had.

When Frank's article came out, it caused quite a commotion. His interview with Johnny changed the whole direction of the article. His firm belief that a terrible crime *had indeed* been committed, and his moral outrage at the apparent apathy surrounding it, really put the story on the map. It was lifted out of the realm of "gossip" and given a validity and an urgency it had hitherto lacked. It was now front-page news.

Clubland was all a-twitter. With Michael's guilt a forgone conclusion, his "friends" began peddling their second-hand stories to *Hard Copy* and *American Journal*. Michael was at the dead center of a media maelstrom. Everywhere you looked, every newspaper and magazine, there he was.

And I thought I was sick of him when he was still in town!

Then, one day, the inconceivable happened.

I came home to find none other than *Michael Alig himself*, drinking a Yoo-Hoo on my stoop. Just as calm and natural as can be! As if he wasn't plastered over the pages of every newspaper in town, and there weren't posters for information leading to his whereabouts or arrest on every lamppost in Manhattan.

I hoped against hope that it wasn't Michael, maybe it was just some crazy *doppelgänger*... one of those quirky twists of fate that always seems to happen to people like me and Jimmy Stewart. *Maybe this green-haired boy, who was now doing a bag of heroin on my stoop, was really Michael's long-lost twin brother . . .*

I wasn't about to take any chances, though. I walked right past him, giving him the same curt nod I give to all the strangers doing drugs on my stoop. Then, I tried to make a run for it, a quick dash up to my apartment.

No dice.

"Blaggerty Slog!" he screamed, by way of welcome.

"WHAT ON EARTH ARE YOU DOING HERE?"

"Oh . . . you know . . . slogger blagging . . . scrod-hopping . . . seeing Roger . . . would you like a bump?"

"Wow, Denver must have really changed you—you've never *offered* before! No thanks. Hate the stuff. You know that. I'd just end up carrying a Tupperware bowl full of vomit around with me all day."

WAIT!

WHAT?!

"I mean, why are you in New York? Are you completely out of your mind?"

"Denver's boring. The crack there is really expensive. Keoki's mean. This is where I belong. I figure now is a good time to capitalize on my press and open a new club. Did you see me on *American Journal*?"

He finally gave me that aneurysm that I've been waiting for all these years. I mean, there's "Old School Thinking," *and then there's* **this** *. . . a truly breathtaking train of thought, so blissfully self-destructive, so utterly confident in its sheer stupidity, that it actually succeeds on all levels.*

"I'm going to call it 'Honeytrap,' " he continued, "after the *Daily News* cover story that said Disco 2000 was like a honey trap that *lured in young children,* and I'm having two thousand jars of honey made up for the invitation . . ."

"Where's my Digitalis?" I screamed, as I fell to the ground.

I soon learned the other reason for his return.

And I was livid when I heard about the deal he was cutting with the DEA, to aid them in their bid to incriminate Peter. Just livid. "Trading Gatien's scalp for Angel's torso," as the *Voice* put it.

We had dinner later that night, and I remained terse and aloof throughout most of the meal. I could barely contain my disgust.

"Michael, darling, pass the pepper—your soylent green is a little bland tonight."

A tense silence. So I changed the subject:

"I read in the *Enquirer* today there's a new fad in Bosnia you might want to get in on. Teenagers collecting noses from the corpses killed in their war-torn homeland. They dry them in the sun to preserve them and string them into necklaces. You didn't by any chance preserve Angel's nose, did you?"

More silence. So I kept at it.

"I'm sorry to keep *harping* on it, but I can't stop thinking about it. Tell me again—*how decomposed was the body when you threw it into the river?* And what do you suppose it looks like now? Are there crawdads in the Hudson? *Do you think the crawdads have gotten to him by now?* What about lampreys? Surely, there are lampreys attached to him, *sucking at the gristle.* And giant mollusks, leeches . . ."

"Stop it, James."

"Are flounder carnivorous by nature? What about smelt? Thousands of tiny smelt just nipping away . . . Well, he's probably not even in the river anymore. Ol' Barnacle Face is probably halfway to Borneo by now . . ."

"Why are you being so mean to me all of a sudden? You're my best friend, you're supposed to help me! You're supposed to understand me! It's not like I'm enjoying any of this!"

"Oh?"

Silence.

"You don't enjoy the ten pages in *Details*? The daily 'Michael Sightings' on 'Page Six'? The David LaChapelle photo shoot? The BBC video crew following you? Anthony Haden-Guest tripping over himself to include your every quip in his book?"

"NO, I DON'T," he said emphatically, an obvious lie because I could see he was getting hard just thinking about it all.

"And you don't think you should be punished in any way for all of this?"

"No. It was an accident. It's not like I'm ever going to do it again."

"Got it all out of your system in one shot, huh?"

"Really. It's not like I'm a *menace to society* . . ."

"An *annoyance* to society, yes."

"James, I'm serious!"

"So am I."

Well, let's just get it out in the open:

"And you don't feel bad about selling out Peter, *PETER*, **Michael,** who has been your best friend, your father, your protector, your benefactor . . . ?"

"I'm just fighting back. And what choice do I have? THIS IS MY LIFE WE'RE TALKING ABOUT. And *they* made the first offer. I would be stupid not to cooperate."

"I just think it's wrong. So wrong. You're a stool pigeon and that's the lowest of the low. *You ought to hang your head in shame.* You LOVED Peter, Michael. **You're guilty,** *you are covered with guilt!* And for you to destroy MORE lives, and knock down everyone around you, and then just walk away from it all with a smile and a 'skroddle doo' in your heart . . . IS WRONG!"

"So you want me to go to prison for life."

"I don't think your freedom should come at Peter's expense. And, yes, I do think you have to somehow pay for what you've done. You have to understand the enormity of your actions."

"You don't think I understand? You don't think I don't think about it *every minute of every day?* You don't think I *wish to God it never happened?* My life is over. It's never going to be the same again. Look at how I'm living: I'm broke, homeless, nobody will hire me. I can't afford my heroin habit . . . I just want to die. I just want to OD and end it all right now."

He was too emotional for me to point out that his regret wasn't *that Angel was dead,* but that his life was in shambles because of it—and that's a fundamentally different *mea culpa.*

"I just wish you would have left the country with Rudolf. I just wish you didn't feel this was your only choice. And how *fucked* is a system that would overlook a *murder . . .*"

". . . an *accident . . .*"

". . . a *dead body . . .* in its zealousness to convict a nightclub owner. I just don't get it."

I had already planned on leaving New York, something I had decided a few months ago. My lease was up in September anyway. I just wouldn't renew.

I just couldn't go on living in a city with so little compassion, so little regard for morality. I needed to live someplace that gives a person some dignity and a little respect for his life . . .

So I was moving to L.A.

Because I was leaving, and felt I owed Michael a generous goodbye, I went on one of his patented club kid jaunts, to a club in Denver for a party that he had set up when he was hiding out there.

Trips with Michael were always excruciating exercises in stress management. This one was beyond comprehension. *You have no idea how difficult it was for me . . .*

He forgot to bring enough heroin to last the week. He did it all on the plane going there. That left seven nonstop days and nights of regret.

It began within hours of arrival.

"Help me—I can't do this! I want to die . . ."

He was doubled over, strictly for my benefit. The tears were real, but it was the junkie glamour of it all, and the attention it could bring, that was the real motivation.

I tried to be helpful, tossing out a few "poor baby"s and a feeble pat on the head now and again—but, truthfully, I was bored by it. And, Lord knows, empathy is not my strong suit.

"James, really, you have to help me," he pleaded. "Go

downtown and cop some for me—you know I'd do it for you."

We were in Denver, for God's sakes, I didn't even know where "downtown" was, much less the regional copping etiquette. They see a wrinkled old white queen toddling around their alleyways—"Begging your pardon, sirs, but I would be much obliged if I could purchase some *horse* from you . . ."

—well, I'm sure I would last all of ten minutes.

So there was much wailing and gnashing of teeth. He yowled and howled and sobbed until there was quite a large crowd of ravers, all clucking and cooing over the poor little monster. He conned fifty dollars out of them, and we were off.

We jumped into a cab.

He directed the van driver to go to the worst corner of the worst part of the city.

"And that would be . . . where?"

"Oh, I don't know. Look for a lot of niggers."

Then he leaned his head out of the van and sang, "NIG-GER-LA-DA-DOOS! NIGGER-LA-DA-DOOS!"

In the nick of time, I happened to remember that nigger-la-da-doos despise that particular appellation. "Good Lord, Michael. Get your face inside this minute. Must we **all** die with you? You mean to tell me that we are just going to drive aimlessly around the city looking for random ne'er-do-wells who may or may not be selling heroin?"

But he couldn't answer. He was swaying back and forth, happily singing his little nigger-la-da-doo song.

Onward ho.

"Stop!" he screamed at a particularly seedy intersection.

"James, get out. You're coming with me."

"**Oh no, I'm not.** You're on your own. I am **not** getting beat up or arrested in a strange town just to shut you up."

I got out anyway. Oh, the tyranny of drug addicts!

Michael scampered off. I watched his little green head bob up and down as he chatted amiably with the native riffraff. I prayed for deliverance.

Of course, leave it to Michael to end up with the lowest common denominator in any situation. It never fails. And so it came to pass that I spent the whole of that lovely, sunny day traipsing through the gutters of downtown Denver with a spooky old panhandler named Smelly Mel. Oh, he was just awful. Michael didn't seem to notice the flies crawling out of the man's nose, or the pungent fecal matter clinging to his pants. No, Michael had found a kindred spirit.

Before long the two of them had linked arms and were whispering like coconspirators. "Hurry up, James. Mel here is going to help us."

One hour, and two aromatic cab rides later: the two of them ducked into an abandoned building. A deal went down. He scored.

Thank God.

He came dashing down the street, happily brandishing his good fortune, waving it high above his head for all the officers on the beat to see.

"Oh James, Mel here has graciously offered to share his needles with me. Isn't that sweet of him?" He turned to Mel, "I'd love to! You're a lamb to offer!" and he batted his lashes appealingly.

"Oh for pity's sake, Michael! Come on."

I dragged him back to the hotel.

Now, this was tar, of course, not the pretty powder New Yorkers prefer. It needs to be cooked and injected. Without Mel's needle, he became frantic.

"How are you at stitching up a gushing artery, James?"

"A little out of practice. Why?"

"I'm going to slash open my wrist and push it directly into my vein. Do you think it will absorb into the bloodstream?"

Thank God I talked him out of *that*. Instead he managed to locate a local faghag who came to his rescue and supplied him with a set of works. Funny, that no matter where you are in the world, there's always someone eager to help you destroy yourself.

It was almost time for me to leave for the airport. Michael had decided to stay another few days, but I had had enough. I packed my things and headed for the door. I turned to say goodbye.

The last time I ever saw Michael, he was blissfully inserting a needle into his arm.

"Bye, Skrink . . ."

"Yea . . . see ya, Skrod . . ."

It was September and the lease was up on my apartment. I was finally free to move, I packed up all of my lovely things—my skrinkles, my skroddles . . . three **full buckets** of hoo-has . . . and *fourteen pairs of flambiggy wignuts!* Twelve years of memories, stuffed into 172 cardboard boxes and tossed into the U-Haul . . . then, I was off!

I wasn't sad. I wasn't angry. I just wanted out of the ugliness.

I clutched my throat and whispered: "Take me away from all this death."

(Actually, I didn't say that. Winona Ryder said it in *Bram Stoker's Dracula*. But it's a good line, and I do a *marvelous* imitation. In fact people often mistake me for her ... No really. *We have the same soulful eyes* ...)

But yea, that's what I was thinking: "Take me away. Get me the fuck out."

New York was on its last leg anyway. After Peter Gatien's clubs were seized by the DEA, and Peter himself was arrested, there was another one of those yawning chasms in nightlife. Another "Death of Downtown." This time, though, there was no new Michael Alig to roar in and shake everything upside down and bring it all back to life. There was no crazy new scene to take the place of the old one. Just a mind-numbing succession of paint-by-number nightclubs, and a few rickrack club kids going through the motions. The fun people just stopped going out. And the ones who kept at it, did so with a drowning man's ferocity, and a hara-kiri, *Blood & Guts* approach to nightclubbing. Of course, since then, most of them have died.

Hey ho.

The world goes on.

So I left New York, I drove to my mother's house and deposited the 172 boxes of crap that I was determined to reclaim someday. God bless Mom, huh? Aren't mothers just wonderful? Mine was a perfect goddess, the entire vacation. She never once pried into my reasons for leaving. She never pressured me to explain about the nights when I still woke up screaming, and the days when I would do nothing but sit in the backyard and laugh at the grass. She knows that something hurt me, and when I'm ready, maybe I'll try to explain it all to her. But in the meantime, she did what she could. She made her signature heart-shaped meatloaf, frosted with red mashed potatoes. That always cheers me up. And she found lots of excuses to give me hugs.

I was still there when I heard the news that a homeless woman who had been fishing for her dinner in the Harlem River had snagged a rotting, limbless torso instead.

The papers all reported that it was Angel's body—recovered at long last!

It took an enormous amount of energy and effort to call Michael and ask what was really going on, but I did. He was doing fine. He was still living at the Chelsea with Brooke. Yes, he'd heard about it. In fact, he was taken in for questioning again. But he seemed completely nonplussed by it all.

"So she hooked herself an Angel-fish, huh?" he said and then laughed himself silly. The rest of the conversation was a bizarre new riff on the Logger Blagger variations. I didn't care enough to decode it.

The body they found turned out *not to be* the body formerly belonging to Angel Melendez. Michael knew that all along. *The police's body* was *armless* as well as *legless*. Michael hadn't been quite so barbaric as to chop off *ALL* of Angel's appendages. *He has his limits* . . . So, this poor, nameless quad was two arms shy to play the lead "amputee-murder victim" in OUR little melodrama.

Sorry, Bob. But, back you go!

(I'm sorry, too. I couldn't resist that. I mean, *what else do you* call an armless and legless body found in the water?) (I have waited **my whole life** to have an excuse to tell that joke, and really, honestly mean it. Oh, that felt good.)

So, they tossed their body back into the river. I guess. Or gave it back to the homeless lady for lunch. "Here you go, ma'am. Sorry about the mix-up."

Just another case of mistaken torso.

Common error.

Could have happened to anyone, and quite frequently does.

About two months after that, the Staten Island police decided to, *oh, maybe look around the station house a bit . . .* see what they might see . . . maybe do a little light dusting, *who knows what might turn up . . .*

And . . .

Lo and behold!

Would you look at that?

Was that what I think it was?

Hm.

Huh.

Goddamn! If it wasn't an unidentified corpse! Right there! Under their very noses, all this time!

Well, I'll be jiggered.

Gee . . . great . . . I mean, *whew!* . . . but . . . well . . . hmmm . . .

I mean . . . isn't it, well, *kind of odd* . . . that they never noticed it there before? . . . I mean, of course . . . well *of course* there's an explanation!

Let's see . . . It was probably just *so busy* the day they fished it out. *See, look here,* they never even had time to take him out of the box and look him over! Did they even remember finding him that day? "Why sure! I remember it well, sir. *There must have been hundreds of bodies washing up, you know how Mondays are, right after the weekend and all!*" . . . Yea. That's what must have happened. So, in that case, wouldn't it be rather selfish of *each corpse* to expect *personal attention?*

Then, of course there was, let's see, Memorial Day . . . then summer . . . *and who really wants to spend the day with an old rotting piece of meat when it's ninety-five in the shade!* I'm serious! **It was a**

perfectly . . . normal . . . oversight. . . . Apparently, they had
only had Angel's remains there, on ice, since when? April?

This was December.

Work with me here, people!

The Staten Island police tried to explain *how it was* that
they had the body all along and never knew it:

"Er . . . uh . . . Mr. Melendez's body washed up here on
Staten Island. It was the Manhattan D.A.'s case. We don't handle
Manhattan cases. That's out of our jurisdiction . . ."

Hello! It's just ANOTHER BOROUGH OF THE SAME CITY,
Boneheads, not fuckin' Timbuktu! *Just how difficult* is it to coordi-
nate bodies in this town?

"And . . . uh . . . we thought the corpse was an Asian person judging from his skin tone."

OK . . . let me see if I got this right—*judging from his skin
tone*—which probably would have been somewhere between
"seafoam" and **"azure"** by that point—*they deduced he was
Asian* . . .

So . . . what? . . . they don't ID dead Asians in Staten Island?

I don't understand.

"Here Sarge! I found two more dead gooks, floating in the
drink!"

"Toss 'em in Lost and Found!"

Oh.

Poor Mother Melendez.

The truth of the matter is: the police just didn't care about
Angel. Not one lick. Because he was a drug dealer. Because he
was Hispanic. And from the Bronx. Because he was gay. Because
he was a night-crawling freak. Because he may or may not have

been an illegal alien, depending which gossip column you read.

The NYPD didn't care enough about Angel to pursue something as time-consuming and bothersome as the truth. Just like everybody else.

I used to joke with Michael that the D.A.'s office probably had a *whole file* of gay drug dealers that they were just DYING to give to him. "Have at it, kid. Here's your hammer, what's your hurry? Don't worry about us. *Ve know nossing! NOSSING!"*

Of course the police knew all along that there were two wacky faggots out there, named Michael and Freeze, who had killed someone named Angel, who used to dress up like a bird, and sell drugs at nightclubs. How could they **not** know? Michael Alig was THE MOST INEPT CRIMINAL OF ALL TIME! Talk about your "fear of success"! He was on autodestruct from the get-go. *He confessed to anybody that would listen. He told the press where his hideout was when he was leaving town. He bungled detail after mind-blowing detail during the actual crime.* And then held a press conference afterward to confirm all of his fuck-ups. . . . Apparently, one time (now I can't verify this, but it certainly sounds possible to me) he had people over, and the box, with the body in it, was out in the living room, *and people used it to set their drinks on all night long!* . . . Oh, Lord help him! . . . He spoke openly and explicitly about the murder *on a phone line that he already suspected to be tapped* (by the DEA, trying to get the goods on Peter). . . . Then he left a paper trail of money a mile long. . . . He even saved all the receipts from his purchases made with the stolen loot!

Another joke I used to say to him was: "Darling, for your next murder, be sure to videotape it for *Hard Copy.* I mean, *you might as well make some money off of it, as long as you've gotten away with it.* Cindy Adams is marvelous, as far as she goes, darling, but she doesn't pay the legal fees."

Hmmm. These aren't very funny jokes when I tell them to *you*. Why is that, do you suppose?

It's certainly clear to me: Michael went out of his way to get caught. He wanted the truth to come out. HE WENT TO LIMELIGHT ONE NIGHT, WITH "GUILT" *ACTUALLY WRITTEN ALL OVER HIS FACE!!!* But for nine months, it looked as if he couldn't even get a traffic ticket in Manhattan. I don't think his silly little murder mattered much until it began to impinge upon THE REALLY IMPORTANT BUSINESS of closing down Peter Gatien's nightclubs! Remember, until then, every reporter who did a story on Michael would call the D.A. and ask for updates on how they were handling the case.

"Case? What case? We got no case. We got better things to do, buddy!"

Yea. More important things. Like spying on people over the bathroom stall doors, while they try, in vain, to urinate!

And picking on poor little drag queens, who, through no fault of their own, just happen to be lying face down on the sidewalk, K'ed out of their freakin' skull.

Sheese!

But I digress.

So they found Angel's body, right there in the police station. Freeze was picked up first for questioning, and immediately JUST BROKE DOWN AND GAVE A COMPLETE WRITTEN STATEMENT. Right there and then.

"Complete" being a relative term.

Like, after reading it, I don't believe it's the "complete" truth. I don't think he's being "completely" honest.

But then, I no longer believe Michael's account either.

I'm convinced they're both lying.

And the truth lies somewhere between the two stories. But we'll probably never know.

Here: Judge Freeze's version for yourself. Don't let me influence you in any way, shape, or form.

You decide.

It's all up to you.

Not me. I'll stay out of it.

Here goes:

CONFESSION

It starts off on a pert note:

On a Sunday in March of 1996 I was at home in my bedroom with a friend.

[This is Freeze's only mention of Daniel.]

In the other bedroom Michael Alig and Angel Melendez were loudly arguing. I, at one point, heard a little crash like glass breaking. Then, I heard the argument progressing and getting louder. I opened the door to the room and started towards the other bedroom. I stopped just outside the bedroom door at which point Michael was yelling "Help me! Get him off of me!" Angel briefly turned and said "Stay out." Then, he grabbed

*Michael either by the shoulder or around the neck and started
shaking him violently and banging him against the wall. He
was yelling "You better get my money or I'll break your neck"—
or something to that effect. I remember Michael looked right at
me with a sort of pleading look in his eyes.*

[This part I love. Michael has that pleading look in his
eyes, so what do you do?]

*I grabbed the hammer which was in the closet directly to my
left.*

[Of course you did. Who wouldn't do exactly the same
thing? Then what did you do, dear?]

*I stepped forward and hit Angel over the head, trying to get
him off of Michael and maybe knock him unconscious.*

[And you did an admirable job of it, at that. You were obviously worried about your dear friend, Michael. We should all
be so lucky to have a Freeze in our life, for just these types of moments . . .]

*I was in a panic and very concerned at the level of anger Angel
was displaying.*

[Sure, sure . . . makes perfect sense to me . . . and nicely
put, too.]

*After the first blow, he turned and grabbed for the hammer. He
might have gotten his hands on it. I'm not sure, but I snatched
it back and hit him in the head again.*

JAMES ST. JAMES

[Get ready for some side-splitting antics here.]

He started to go down, but he was still pissed off

[Well, who wouldn't be? Can't fault the guy for that one . . .]

and he started going for Michael again. So, I hit him a third time and he went down. At this point, Michael got onto his chest and was strangling him with his hands. I yelled "What are you doing?" Michael seemed to be very angry at this point and was cursing at Angel. He then took a pillow and put it over Angel's face. I made him stop by either telling him to stop or pushing him off of Angel.

[Let me pause and wipe the tears of laughter from my eyes. But wait, it gets better.]

I then walked into the livingroom, and possibly to the bedroom.

[?]

When I returned, Michael was beside the body again. I noticed a broken syringe on the floor by the body, and Michael was pouring something from the bathroom, some cleaner or chemical, into Angel's mouth. I, again screamed, "What are you doing? What is your problem? He's out!"

[Freeze, the innocent bystander, voice dripping with concern: "What are you doing? You might hurt Angel!"]

He then started wrapping tape around his mouth. He asked for the duct tape from the closet and said "You have to help me!"

PARTY MONSTER

[So what did you do, Freeze?]

So, I helped him finish wrapping the tape around Angel's mouth.

[I wouldn't have expected anything less.]

Then I left the room. When I came back Angel was undressed down to his underwear, a pair of white "Fruit of the Loom" type underwear.

[Such pleasant imagery: a mangled, taped-up corpse in his underwear. Make that a mangled, taped-up corpse in his **white "Fruit of the Loom"-type underwear**—it makes all the difference when you think about it.]

Michael said "Help me put him into the tub." So we carried him to the tub, and closed the bathroom door.

[Here comes an all-time classic line:]

About 5–7 days later, Michael and I decided we had to do something about this terrible mess.

[Can we all take a moment and howl over this one? "Five ... to ... seven days later ..." Don't you just hate it when time just slips away from you? So much to do, the days pass by in a drugged-out haze, and you forget there's a stinking blue body in the bathtub ...]

It was decided that I would go to get knives or something to help dispose of the body. I went to Macy's and bought 3 large knives; 2 chef knives and 1 cleaver. When I got back Michael told me that if I gave him 10 bags of heroin he would take care of this part. So I did and he went into the bathroom alone, and cut off both of Angel's legs. Then, we put each leg into plastic bags, and then a duffel bag and seperately carried them, one at a time, to the river and threw them in. Probably about the next day I went downstairs to the storage area and got a large box. I cut the UPC code off the box. I brought it up to the apt. Michael put the remainder of the body into a large plastic garbage bag. I got another bag and put it over the first one. I think before Michael put it in the first bag, he wrapped it in a sheet. After the second bag I think I taped it closed. We then put the whole bundle into the large box.

[Angel shall henceforth be known as "The Bundle." I like that.]

The smell was so unbearable that I put baking soda in to absorb (hopefully) some of the odor. I also stuck a broom handle into the box for support because the sheer weight was making the box collapse. A few hours later we took the box into the elevator and out through the main lobby into a yellow cab that happened to be right outside the door. The driver helped to tie the trunk down and we took the body to the Westside Highway around 25th Street.

[Across the street from the Tunnel.]

The taxi drove off, and we threw the box into the river.

This statement was written by me, Robert Riggs, of my own free will, my Miranda rights were also read to me, at this location:

> *84 Wooster St., 7th fl.*
> *N.Y., NY*

PARTY MONSTER

So.

There you have it.

I leave it to you, Gentle Reader, to compare and contrast Michael's original story with Freeze's sworn statement. There are some niggling inconsistencies *(was the Drano swallowed or injected?)*; a few glaring omissions *(like that Michael never even mentioned the pillow incident)*; and what about that slumbering person in the next room? What does he remember?

As for me, well, That's it! I'll just retire gracefully. Fade into the background. This sleuthing thing was never really my style, anyway. My *"Grim and Determined"* look just frightened the children and gave me gas. But, hey, don't let that discourage **YOU** from gathering together, and discussing it amongst yourselves.

This story is not over yet. Not by a long shot.

"DEAR MICHAEL"

So.

How are you doing?

How's prison life?

Oh, before I forget: be a lamb, and give Freeze *a big old bear hug* from me. How nice that his cell is RIGHT ACROSS THE HALL from you! I miss him so much. Why, just the other day, I received the funniest letter from him—*all about Edna Ferber . . .*

Keoki told me the two of you organized all the inmates in a game of *$20,000 Pyramid. I'm so glad you're having fun.*

You really are **so lucky**, Michael. It all sounds **so interesting.** You're at a twenty-four-hour-a-day party, with cute boys and interesting people who have led such *fascinating* lives—why, you couldn't ask for a better setup!

It is so much harder out here in the real world, honey. I

know you wouldn't want to trade places with me. It is **so** difficult to make friends in Los Angeles—everybody is so stand-offish, just so busy doing their own thing! Count your blessings, girl.

Why, I hear that things are going just *swimmingly* with you. Keoki said that you've joined something called the Aryan Nation—doesn't that sound like fun? Are they dancers? And what's this "Prison Protection" thing that you have to pay dues for? Is it a social club?

What fun!

I can see you now, getting all dressed up for meetings and social functions . . . Oh, and the mess hall . . . lunches and dinners with your new friends! Please write and tell me all about it!

You must be pretty happy, huh?

And I was thrilled to hear that you've been reading up on your classics—*what I wouldn't give for ten to twenty worry-free years to do nothing but lounge around and brush up on my Middle English.*

I hear you just read *Crime and Punishment.*

Good for you.

You realize, of course, that if you just changed the names, it could be exactly your story, don't you?

Tell that to Diane Sawyer when she comes 'round next week. Tell her that you were merely testing the old Dostoyevskian Conundrum: if you kill an unlovable cretin, is the crime still as heinous?

It's an interesting question isn't it? Not as cut and dry as you might think. It's shocking to me that everyone we know seems to think that the severity of your crime is somehow lessened because *you* are so beloved and *Angel* was so despised.

There are some, like Keoki , who have just pulled down the shutters in their mind, and refuse to let the truth shine in. You know, he actually looked me in the face yesterday and said: "I don't think Michael really had anything to do with it, do you?"

This, after he's had a whole year to digest it.

Bless his heart. He still wants to believe that you are the same person he met at Area a dozen years ago.

How pathetic.

Then there are others like Gitsie, dear sweet Gitsie, bless her heart. Gitsie, who *just never wanted* to understand what you did. She never really grasped the ethical implications of your murder, did she? She just liked being where the action was. She liked it when people got all excited and talked about *SERIOUS ISSUES.* I honestly believe that during all of those conversations we had in front of her, the only thing running through her head was what color to paint her toenails next. God bless her. It's a shame she died so suddenly like that. Overdosed the day before the trial was set to begin!

Whoops.

And Jenny, what are we going to do with her? She just floats in and out, a moot presence. She doesn't care about anything except "Oh My God, how much homework" she has to do.

And the others? Brooke. Well, she's in prison now, too, thanks to you. But she doesn't hold it against you.

And Jeremy. Bryan. Peter-Peter Boyfriend Stealer. *They're not sorry, they just love you anyway. Whatever it was that you did, they could care less. You make them laugh.* It's as easy as that.

And they have a point.

It's a difficult thing to grasp—this duality that exists in you. On the one hand, you are a wicked, wicked boy—*and you really are Michael, just evil incarnate, sometimes.*

But on the other hand, you're still Michael, that hasn't

changed. You're still funny and charming and worldly and wise. You're still my best friend.

You were always such an inspiration to me, and that's why I was so hurt and angry about all of this.

Sometimes when I would look at you, Michael, from across the bar, or out on the dance floor, I couldn't even see you—*you shone so brightly.* You were a genius. You made my mouth drop. I felt so honored that you treated me as your equal, when so clearly you were always *leaping* and *bounding* far, far ahead of me.

But you failed.

You had so much inside of you and yet you threw it away. *You hadn't finished changing the world, yet.* You should be plotting corporate takeovers, making million-dollar deals, directing feature films, starting your own religion—not sitting in some overcrowded prison cell!

And, if YOU failed, how on earth are the rest of us supposed to succeed?

What are we all supposed to do now?

Remember how you laughed when I told you I was writing a book about all of this madness, remember your comment: **"Isn't that rich?"** you said, **"Isn't that classic?** How dare you, James, co-opt **MY** murder to make yourself look fabulous! Go commit your **OWN** murder and let me have my moment!"

"But, Michael," I protested in my most sincere little Dianne Brill voice, "this whole murder thingie **REALLY... UPSET...ME..."**

And, oh, how you roared at that one. "*I* killed some-one . . . *I'M* in prison . . . but YOU'RE upset—so you get to profit from it. YOU ARE TOO MUCH, JAMES ST. JAMES!"

"Seriously, darling, *let's bottom line it:* . . . you know, and I know, that I am **the only person** left, who can **(or will)** paint a semisympathetic portrait of you . . . And I am **the only person** with the skill and finesse to render *the big dismemberment scene* as a *warm and fuzzy Hallmark moment* that you can proudly tuck into your press portfolio. So how 'bout it? Care to help out your old pal? Cough up some details for me."

You finally relented. After all, I *am* your best friend.

So here we go, one more time. For the record. There are still some things I don't understand.
For instance:
I don't understand how Angel came to be such an impor-tant part of your life to begin with. We *hated* Angel.

I remember the first time I saw the two of you together, in-teracting like friends. It was in December . . . almost three months before the murder . . . at Bowery Bar, for the inaugural meeting of the ten-year-club—one of your last, and most bla-tant, stabs at Old School acceptance. I remember how diligently you identified and categorized each and every bold-faced so-cialite who survived the ten-year mark. You alphabetized and la-beled them. I remember that no one—NO ONE—was allowed entree to this meeting unless they were duly wizened and could honestly remember our old *alma mater:* Area.
They were all rewarded—for slathering on the pancake makeup and discussing archaic clubland politics with you—

with three free dinners at Bowery Bar and a truly cheerless party at the Limelight. What a *marvelous* opportunity for you to parade around and show all those various VIP-vaulting cronies how gracefully you were entering the twilight of your club-kidding years!

You looked a bit peaked to be sure (shooting up will do that to you), but isn't it amazing how a little soap and water on the face and some laundry detergent in the wash can make all the difference? I don't think I'd seen you this pressed in YEARS! It must have been so important for you to make a good impression...

Which is why we were all so shocked when you arrived with Freeze and Angel. If you remember correctly, the rest of us were strictly denied ANY guests of any type. "No riffraff," you said. "Just old friends." (This despite the fact that none of them were really our old friends, and most likely, WE were the riffraff they avoided.)

Angel and Freeze had not been around ten years, darling. And neither one of them was what you might call "a dazzling conversationalist." And Angel with those silly wings—oh Michael, really—weren't you embarrassed to be seen with him?

Obviously not. When you took your place at the head of the table, you had HIM sit at your right-hand side—traditionally a seat of honor, according to Miss Manners.

Hello! What is wrong with this picture, Michael? Dianne should have been at your right. Or Sylvia Miles.

I don't remember that *sour old milksop* at Area, do you? I don't remember his **tanjy-ass** at any of the **Andy Warhol dinner parties** that I ever went to! Just looking across the table at that *molten little scavenger* dressed up for all the world like a *syphilis-ridden carrier pigeon*... oh, it made my blood boil!

And watching the attention that you lavished on him...!

Well, I wasn't the only guest who was miffed, we'll put it that way. As I sat with the rest of the has-beens, in the section of the table known as "Siberia," watching the two of you just *draped* on top of each other, each one of you just as *smug as a bug*, it was a **truly nauseating spectacle** to behold—*that's what we all said to each other*—"Why, it's nauseating to behold."

I mean, who blessed this unholy union of tack and greed, anyway?

And look at just how **eager** he was to lick your elderly butthole! Disgusting!

"Grizzle and Grovel"—that's who the two of you were! That's what I said, and, my, **how we all** laughed at that one!

That's when you came over to our section.

I had to wipe me mouth when ya kissed me, WIPE ME MOUTH! (*Spit*)

Then you leaned into my ear and whispered—"Really, James, if you want any K you have to be nicer to Angel."

Why, oh *why*, must we always go through pigs to get our truffles?

So I smiled and went over and gave Angel a big kiss, then a hug too. And I sat and chatted with him for a **whole twenty minutes!** *But let me just say* **this** *about* **that;** it took an entire half gram of cat tranquilizer to get that image out of my head, yes siree, Bob. An entire half gram to forget what an ass we made of ourselves that night.

That was the beginning, wasn't it? I knew it then. I know it now.

Pretty soon the three of you were seen everywhere together. You and Freeze and Angel.

Just as thick as thieves!

And speaking of thievery, Michael: how was it that you and Freeze first convinced him to leave his money and drugs at your apartment, anyway? Had he taken COMPLETE leave of his senses? What, did the two of you hypnotize him? Were you holding his mother hostage? I don't get it. Why would someone as *stingy* and *cynical* as Angel was (and we all know what a painful skinflint he was, really just impossible), why would he give you two snarf-monsters ALL OF HIS DRUGS AND ALL OF HIS MONEY every night for safe keeping?

Did he think that y'all were *friends?*

But somehow you did it.

I commend you—it's a credit to our kind. Separating a dealer from his drugs AND his money?! In such grand quantities?! Over such an extended period of time?!

Good show, old chap. Really. Bully for you!

You and Freeze had *carte blanche,* didn't you? You had the keys to yet another candy store, didn't you, hon?

And that's when things really flew out of control.

I stopped by your apartment in January for some reason; I can't recall why. I do remember that we hadn't seen much of each other lately. I had been avoiding you and Freeze. *That needle thing was just so unattractive . . .* And those open wounds of yours, all up and down your legs . . . It almost made me want to stop doing drugs altogether.

Yes, it did! I am not kidding.

You were still with that awful boyfriend of yours, Noel.

Remember him?

Beautiful!

Just beautiful!

Stunning features . . .

Could have been a supermodel.

Except for that disturbing habit he had of **shooting up everything in sight.**

Remember when he shot up the bottle of chardonnay?

Now, **that'll** draw some disapproving stares from the *maître d'*, I'll tell you that much.

Each and every time.

Some people will do *anything* for a bit of a buzz!

Anyway, when I came over, you were combing your hair with a fork and you offered me an eightball of cocaine. I did it, even though **YOU KNOW** how much I hate cocaine. It's the Devil's candy. I just despise it.

But there I was, all jacked up, watching you comb your hair with a fork. And I couldn't take my eyes off those big old paws of yours. Those big old oven mitts that you call hands. I sat and **really looked at them** and remembered that the *more fucked up you are, the more heroin you do, the drier and scalier your hands get.* Isn't that odd?

Well, my Lord, Michael, you had the hands of a Gila monster. You must have been on a *three-month bender* to get them as **crackled** and **chapped** as they were!

Then every once in a while, you would *swipe your claw* at one of the *pus-filled, open wounds* on your legs—I swear to God, it was like watching the Saturday-morning creature feature! It made me want to vomit.

That's when I realized just how far this ride with Angel was going.

So.

We must have done another eightball, which meant that we had to cook up some of his K. It's really the only way. Once that ugly feeling starts creeping up, God help you if you don't have any K.

Then after doing his K, we felt *very lovely* indeed, and decided to invite a few friends over, and for that we had to dip into Angel's money (to pay for their cabs, of course).

The snow had begun to fall and accumulate on the streets at an alarming rate, until we couldn't see outside. A solid wall of powder had dropped onto the city.

It was a blizzard, and as the hours passed and the drugs disappeared, your friends clomped in, each one louder and more frenetic than the last, until we had gathered a handsome group of junkies to share in Angel's goodwill. Outside, it grew still darker, still whiter, and still more dangerous.

But by now gravity and heroin, those old familiar foes, were pulling at my head. So it was onto the rank and fermenting mattress in your bedroom, joined by the others. There was no going home for any of us. The streets were officially blocked off and New York City was buried alive. Four feet of snow would fall that night, and there were drifts so high, we couldn't see out your balcony door.

There was nothing to do but hunker down for the evening.

It should have been warm and cozy on that bed, with all of us together in a big old tangled pile of drug-withered arms and legs. It should have been all sweetness and cuddles.

In fact, you toasted with a bump of heroin—an easy, breezy platitude about friendship and togetherness. And we all inhaled and said, "Here, here." But somehow I didn't feel it.

In fact I heard a voice that wasn't quite my own, come out of my mouth and say something very odd.

I heard myself say that "I don't think I've ever really been happy"—but of course that's ridiculous, not something I would ever say at all. *Of course* I've been happy, **loads of times.** In fact, I was happy just a few minutes ago.

But there it was.

"I don't think I've ever been happy," said in a far-off voice, one that sounded old and nostalgic for a moment that hadn't yet passed; nostalgic for today, even as I lived it. It was strangled and tight, and not coming from anywhere inside my head. A voice from far away, maybe here and now, reaching back and telling me it wasn't real, the years we had, the times we had, the feeling of belonging, none of it was real. Soon, very soon, it would be ripped away. Soon, too soon, I was going to be tumbling and falling with you, and we both would feel the pain of separation, of being taken away from everything that we worked so hard to build.

But as I said the words—"I don't think I've ever been happy"—it wasn't time yet, we were still together, alive, free. It was odd and wrong coming from my throat like it did.

So you waved your hand and dismissed it at once, as you are so often wont to do.

"Tut, tut, my dear. Maudlin crap."

"No time for cheap sentiment."

For someone so hell-bent on recapturing the past, you have a surprisingly low tolerance for the nostalgia of others.

As my gloomy rumination still hung in the air, there was a gust of wind and a shadow fell on the wall. It was Angel.

How he got through the storm, and why he was there, on a Monday night, when the city was shut down and the streets were unmanageable, was anybody's guess.

But there he was, and for a moment we all looked guilty—

because, of course, we were—we were caught with our noses in the cookie jar, and it didn't look good.

Er . . . uh . . .

Humina, humina, humina . . .

But you just smiled and batted your eyelashes. "Oh, uh, we, uh, justdidallyourcocaineandthreegramsofK."

Angel didn't seem to mind. "Whatever. We'll figure it out later."

"You're on the budget for Wednesday and Saturday."

You are SO GOOD at it. Hats off.

Funny that he was so understanding **then** . . . when just a month later, the two of you *came to blows* over the amount of money that you owed him. That was the first time he ever stood up to you, wasn't it? In fact, it was probably the first time **any** club kid ever stood up to you.

I can only guess how much you must have stolen from him that time, and what sort of debt you must have accumulated— *you must have just pushed him about as far as he could go.* Imagine Angel (!) getting up the nerve to push **YOU!** Hit **YOU!** Question your absolute authority! When he appeared to worship the ground you walked on!

But he did. He pushed you. He hit you and you fought back. The whole scene talked of nothing else for days. That's how you got that nasty bruise on your neck, right? Or was that a lie, too? Setting up the alibi, hmmm?

That was near the end of February, just a week or two before you slaughtered him.

Don't you wish now that first scuffle had been the end of the relationship? That he would have packed up his things and left your sorry old junkie-ass when he had the chance? Then he would be alive, and you would be free, and the rest of us could sleep nights without the weight of all this self-righteous indignation bearing down upon us.

I called you a few days after the fight, and Angel picked up the phone.

"What on *earth* are you still doing at that house?" I asked.

"Oh . . . you know."

"No, I am sure that I don't know, Mister. You are an *idiot* to stay there. What possesses you?"

He ignored my comment. "Michael and Freeze are at Bowery Bar right now."

"Tell them I called. And really, Angel, think about what a fool you're being."

Click.

That was the last time I spoke to him. Those were my last words to him. "You're an idiot. You're a fool. Why are you in that house?"

I told him to get out. Call me Cassandra, but I knew something was wrong. I wish I could say, "I told you so." I wish I could laugh in his face.

But of course, it's too late.

They never listen, do they?

On Sunday, March 31st, I wandered out of Club Expo into an unseasonably late snowstorm. I stumbled around Times Square, lost in an industrial strength K-hole, for close to an hour, without my shoes on. Somehow I found my way to your house, where I thought I would be safe and everything would be all right.

That's when you served me tea and scones and a little dollop of heroin and told me that you had butchered Angel and tossed him in the Hudson River.

So much for warmth and safety.

"Does this change how you think of me?" you asked, that night when you told me.

"Do you still love me?" you asked.

And when I said that nothing could ever be the same for me anymore, that I could never be happy just dressing up and going out, that I could never find joy in nightclubbing ever again—well, you started crying so hard you got hiccups.

And you hugged my knees and said that was the worst thing I could have ever said—that that was the one thing you never wanted to take away from me.

How silly that would sound to anybody who was listening! How superficial to say that because of a murder, I didn't feel like dressing up anymore! That I didn't want to go to parties anymore!

I now know that you CAN'T just make up your own rules. And you CAN'T just live in your own little world.

Easy stuff for everybody else.

Suddenly, at age twenty-nine, I had to face the fact that the lines were drawn on the road because it was *best for everyone that way.*

Your example taught me what I thought I would never find in myself: that to endure you must live within society's structure, and work with it, and join in the rest of the world.

So, if it's superficial that my response to your murder is to stop wearing false eyelashes—**then goddamnit**—SO BE IT.

And, you know, finally, when all is said and done: God Bless Angel.

GOD FUCKING BLESS ANGEL.

Can we just say that?

Can we just get that out there *once and for all?*

Can we just acknowledge his passing and mourn for a moment?

He never knew what hit him, did he?

He never knew how short the ride was. He hadn't experienced life yet—how could he understand **death** when it came for him?

I don't think anyone will ever know what really happened that day. I don't think I even care anymore.

Sometimes at night, I see the shadow of your claw. I hear the beating of wings, and there is a sudden spray of blood upon the wall. A breath stops, and with it goes somebody's world. Feathers fall gently to the ground and there is a close-up of your smiling blue face, with those awful red polka dots.

Angel is gone.

I'm back there again and I'm always there and I can never leave.

Now, I don't believe that the conscious mind can survive death. But I pray that something lasts, and I hope that somewhere in this world there is something left of him.

And if there isn't, then I'm going to make it up, and I'm going to make it so. I'm hanging on to a piece of light and I'm going to let it live forever.

Happy re-birthday, Angel.

EPILOGUE

Suddenly, I was thirty.

Suddenly I was this **cranky old clam** with a **flat ass** and **hairballs in my ear.** Suddenly my age-defying makeup, didn't. I was old and all alone in a strange new town. And when I looked in the mirror for comfort? Why, there was some strange **leathery old faggot** staring back at me with yellow, rheumy eyes.

Where was that strapping young buck of yore?

My face was cracking, my boobs were sagging, and I smelled like sour milk. Decomposition must be setting in early! Was that a hunchback I saw forming? The heartbreak of scoliosis?

I was a mess!

How could this happen to me?

ME!

Why, just yesterday, it seems, I was leaping off bar stools and dancing on tabletops with all the insouciance of youth. I was unwrinkled then, and happy. The world was my oyster . . .

Then—

POW! BANG!

One little murder and I go off the deep end! Next thing I know, I'm this grizzled old she-hag, dry-humping the cigarette machine. Prunella Turkeyneck!

Ah! Youth!

Fleeting, fading, slipping away!

What is one to do?

Endure, of course.

So, as I roll toward middle age, leaving yesteryear behind—who really cares if I look like **Christina** and my **testicles are knocking against my knees?**

Who cares if I have nothing to look forward to except a slow, debilitating, downward spiral?

And realistically looming in my future? Bedpans, liver spots, and ear trumpets.

Well, what of it?

There is nothing sad or pathetic about my decay. Look at me. Really look at me—drag this old monster into the light. Poke me with your pitchforks. I will not shrink from your scrutiny! I am James St. James. I am like the Parthenon—something once great, fallen into ruin!

But I can still stop traffic, goddamnit.

As I prepare to enter my dotage (please call me **Dame** St. James from now on), I check the mirror for gout, put on a pretty gray wig, and a lacey little shawl, and powder my face with a bit of talcum . . . but darlings, I am not yet going to retire, Miss Havisham–like to the attic.

I am leaving the safety of my home and going to find my manifest destiny.

With my heavily veined and frail, bony hands, I clutch my walker and head for the door. It takes me ten minutes to walk the twenty-six steps to the elevator—*oh, won't somebody please pumice my corns for me?* Then another forty-four steps to the front door of the lobby, where I paused to hock up a phlegmball the size of a Hacky Sack. I consider going back, but then I catch a whiff of hydrangea on the wind, and it spurs me out into the sunlight.

Oh! Los Angeles! My home?

I kick a palm frond from my path, then reflect how nicely it would look rising out of my wig—*did I have a couple dozen bobby pins tucked into my clutch?* Oh, how the kids would go crazy for that look at Limelight . . . if only Limelight was still around. At least that nice Mr. Gatien got off. Acquitted of all charges! Good for him.

I pluck a hibiscus flower and place it behind my ear, instead. I reapply my lipstick in the rearview mirror of a parked pickup truck.

Well, *would you look at me!*

The old girl's got some snap in her garter yet!

I looked like one of those *Far Side* women, with the cornflower sunglasses, wobbly jowls, and elbow fat! What fun!

It was another 268 steps to the corner bakery. *Yumpin' Yimminy!* Look at those young'uns **dashing** across the street— you'd think they were lemmings! It's a wonder they make it through the day!

At Manii's Bakery, I take my time and look over all the delicious goodies. Lemon Torte! Pecan Praline! Oh, what I wouldn't give for some ribbon candy!

Would you look at the *precious expressions* on those gingerbread men?

It's a shame I never had grandchildren!

I choke back a wistful tear.

Thirty years old, and still no grandchildren!

Then I see what I came for. I asked the nice young man behind the counter for a single slice of Cinnamon Raisin Swirl.

I looked at it long and hard and thought of Michael and of all of the years we spent together.

Then I shove it all in my mouth at once, and swallow without even chewing.

The other customers gape at me.

"What are you staring at? You've never seen a man in a muumuu before? What's the matter? Are my Depends sagging? Go back to your muffins, all of you!"

And with that, I *tossed* my walker aside, *sprang* for the door, and *bolted head first into traffic.*

Goodbye Michael.

Hello World.

Acknowledgments

My deepest and most heartfelt appreciation goes out to everyone involved with *Party Monster.*

To Randy Barbato and Fenton Bailey—without you I'm nothing. Thank you, thank you, thank you. You gave me my life back.

To my agents William Clark and Cat Ledger—without your enthusiasm and conviction, I'd probably still be lying in a mud puddle somewhere.

To my editor at Simon & Schuster—Chuck Adams, an angel, an honest to God angel, who really understood where I was coming from and helped guide me through the tough spots.

To Ed Davis, my lawyer, for . . . for . . . being so damned thorough.

To everyone at World of Wonder, especially Thairin, Tiffany, Karin, Ed, Scott, and Harry.

To all the Downtown Superstars who give the scene its magic: Kenny Kenny, Richie Rich, Sophia LaMar, Amanda La-Pore, Astro Earle, Julie Jewels, Walt Paper, Robert and Tim Twin, J.J., Sushi, Sacred, Desire, Tobell, Cody, and Brie. I love you all. I miss you all.

To Michael Musto and Stephen Saban, thank you for your friendship and support.

And to Rickie, Rickie, Rickie. It's always all for you.

About the Author

James St. James, who was once dubbed a "celebutante" by *Newsweek* magazine, now leads a quiet, sedate existence in Los Angeles, far from the madness that he writes about. This is his first book.